In The Beginning:

A New Theory of the First Religion

Edward Conklin Ph.D.

ISBN 978-0-9906457-2-6

Acknowledgments

I gratefully acknowledge and thank family, friends, and teachers for their encouragement. I also acknowledge and thank and am indebted to the many Paleolithic researchers who have come before and without whose tireless efforts and findings this work could not have been written.

Published works by Edward Conklin Ph.D.

A Brief Guide to God and the Soul. (2015). Amazon Kindle and CreateSpace.

In the Beginning: A New Theory of the First Religion. (2014). Amazon Kindle and CreateSpace.

Cosmos, God, and Soul. (2014). Amazon Kindle and CreateSpace.

From Tool-maker to God Maker. (2014). Amazon Kindle and CreateSpace.

Waves Rough and Smooth & the Deep Blue Sea. (2014). Amazon Kindle and CreateSpace.

Getting Back Into the Garden of Eden. (1998). University Press of America.

Contents

Introduction

This work is a revision of my Ph.D. dissertation completed in 2002 entitled, *The First Religion: Evidence For Its Beginning and Earliest Artistic Expressions.*

Many definitions of the Latin-derived word religion exist today. The basic derivation of the term may be traced to *re* meaning again, and *legere,* meaning connect, literally, "to reconnect." Early humans began to practice religion when they became interested in locating, connecting with, or finding their way back to the origin of life on earth. Many definitions of religion exist; however, my proposed definition is more basic and comprehensive.

While many researchers would be hesitant to seek the presence of religion so long ago, I will argue that, based on three types of artifact remains circa 100,000-6,000 BP, there is evidence of religious thinking and behavior that suggests a concern by early humans for the origin of their existence as well as that of animal and plant life. These areas of evidence are Neanderthal burial, European Paleolithic cave art, and female figures. While other archeological remains such as tools, ornaments, and diet and subsistence patterns do exist, evidence will be presented that these artifacts more than any other early endeavor reveal the human comprehension that the beginning of all life came from within the earth, including plant, animal, and human existence.

I will seek to establish that all three areas are conjoined by a single developed and long lasting geocentric (earth-centered) and gynocentric (female-centered) religious view. Comprehending the dynamics of this primal religious view that endured for nearly 100,000 years can contribute much to a better comprehension of the human condition. It can also lead to an appreciation of the long and poignant human search by forebears that has continued from the Paleolithic era into modern times to discover how all things have come into existence.

Numerous views exist regarding the phenomena of human burials that began with Neanderthals circa 100,000 BP and continued until the extinction of the line circa 28,000 BP. Some of these include the view that the burials were not intentional, (Gargett, 1989) whereas others are convinced the burials were intentional (Kooijmans, et al., 1989). When intentional, views vary as to the intention, ranging from emotional bonds (Chase & Dibble, 1987) to hygiene (Tattersall, 1995; Stringer & Gamble, 1993) and others. Gargett's view ignores convincing evidence of intentional burial by Neanderthals, while views for intentional interment lack grounding in the artifact evidence and often rely on the use of analogy with contemporary tribal cultures. I argue that Neanderthal burials were intentional and that this interaction with the earth indicates a geocentric religious view. Thus, the interring of the human body in the soil of rock-shelters and caves reveals the strategic view that the origin of life came from within the earth.

Neanderthals, having a brain similar to modern humans, had the cognitive capacity for three mostly subconscious as well as conscious mental processes. The first is animism, attributing life to non-living things; the second is anthropomorphism, the mostly subconscious attribution of human characteristics to nonhuman things or processes; and the third occurs during sleep as the vivid imagery of consciously recalled subconscious dreams. While Neanderthals were generally assumed to have not possessed the ability to think and reason, the evidence of differing subsistence patterns suggest planning and the imitative making of 63 kinds of flake tools and 21 variations of the hand-axe, suggest that they were also capable of the conscious process of rudimentary analogical reasoning; in other words, they could have reasoned simply "this is like that." Experiencing and observing the human newborn coming from the opening of and interior of the female body, both Neanderthal genders, through the cognitive processes of animism, anthropomorphism, dreams, and analogical reasoning, were the first humans to perceive and liken or gynocentrically compare this individual event to their group origin from the cave openings and the interior of the earth. In this way, they introduced the earliest and first religion of humankind.

Evidence of this religious idea of the interior of the earth as the origin of life continues with Homo sapiens sapiens from the beginnings of European cave art circa 35,000 BP until the end of this artistic behavior circa 10,000 BP. Numerous theories attempt to explain the existence of Paleolithic cave or parietal art, which is defined as images engraved, drawn, painted, or sculpted on the ceilings, walls, and floors of caves.

The most popular view of researchers is that the cave art was made exclusively by males as an expression of hunting or fertility magic and shamanistic rituals. However, research has shown that less than four percent of the animal depictions have marks on them that could be interpreted as weapons and the images are never portrayed alarmed as a result of being wounded. The fertility magic and shamanistic theories are not convincingly supported by relevant artifact remains and are often speculative and rely on the use of analogy with historic tribal groups.

I will argue that the images of animals, plants, and hand prints were drawn primarily by women as a result of the perceptual processes of animism, anthropomorphism, dream imagery, and the analogically reasoned gynocentric view that the interior of the earth was the female-like greater origin of life. Therefore, the cave images were a "petition" by the artists who acted as "midwives" in assisting the earth to bring forth the portrayed living forms. Just as women made life within the interior of their abdomen and eventually gave birth, so they gathered within the greater interior of caves to petition and assist the earth to bring to life the various animals by engraving and painting likenesses of these living forms. Archeological support for this view is also found in the prevalence of smaller hand prints and footprints left by the artists in a number of caves in France and Spain. This "petitionary-midwife model" also explains an important anomaly in the faunal record for which few previous explanations have been offered or are convincing, regarding the discrepancy between the species of animals depicted in the cave art, and the remains of the animals eaten by the inhabitants.

The third area of evidence of a Paleolithic religion is that of the "Venus figures" produced circa 30,000-12,000 BP. Theories vary for this phenomenon of sculpted and engraved human-like female images. Views include that the figures functioned to increase or glorify human fertility or reproduction, (Giedon, 1962) as a recognition or honoring of womanhood, (Rice, 1982) or even represented a pathological condition of excessive breast development (Harding, 1976).

My findings show that these views are not convincingly supported by the artifact remains, and that they rely exclusively on research obtained from or associated with modern women. The female figures have few facial features, the feet are missing and the hands are often not present. While marked on the Willendorf Venus and a few others, the vulvae are missing from the majority of images, nipples are not indicated on the breasts, and the female figures are never depicted in childbirth, nursing newborns, or with children. Moreover, there is little evidence of clothing. These characteristics strongly prompt a question. Are these Venus figures an accurate image of the human female? The answer would have to be no. The artists omitted the details that would have represented women naturalistically. Lacking these details, which the artists seem quite capable of representing, the Venus figures are generalized human-like images of the body and are not particularly identifiable females.

I argue that these female figurines are not Venus figures; but rather they are planet Earth figures, and are the earliest anthropomorphism of a deity, namely the interior of the earth as the female origin of human, animal, and plant life. The unknown shape of the earth was made known through anthropomorphizing it. The figures are a conceived gynocentric and geocentric combination and expression of the knowledge early humans had of where life originated, inside the human female body and the mysterious interior of the earth.

A final discussion will investigate the rapid decline and demise of the view that the interior of the earth was the origin of life including that of humankind, which, I will argue, is evident in the cessation of the making of the cave art of animal and plant images, and female figures.

Some of the events that contributed to the collapse of the long term geocentric and gynocentric religious view of the Paleolithic people include a changing environment, domestication of animals and plants, and most importantly, the eventual awareness of the male role in the process of reproduction. This comprehension of the male contribution to reproduction is evident in the increasing presence of anthropocentrism and androcentrism in the content of Late Paleolithic, Azilian, and Mesolithic Levantine art.

Chapter 1

Definition of Religion

In seeking evidence of the first religion it is necessary to define the term. However, since there is no general consensus for the definition of religion, this endeavor is problematic. How should the word religion be defined? What are the cognitive processes that have contributed to the development of religion? What evidence is there for the presence of a religious view and practice during the Paleolithic era? In an attempt to answer these questions, I will:

1. Review many definitions of the word religion so as to discern a basic or essential meaning that would apply to religion regardless of time and place.
2. Present a number of religious views as evidence to support my proposed definition of the term religion.
3. Present the innate cognitive processes that have contributed to the development of a religious view and discuss how other prominent theories for religion have failed to adequately comprehend and explain these functions.
4. Examine the artifacts from the Middle and Upper Paleolithic era circa 100,000-10,000 BP for evidence of a religious view and practice during this time.

While some researchers' doubt whether the word can be defined, (Spilka, Hood & Gorsuch, 1985, p. 4; Smith, 1978, p. 17) there exist many definitions of as well as theories about the phenomenon known as religion. There are psychological, mystical, sociological, ethical, political, and even legal (Casino, 1999) definitions of religion.

Definitions of religion that emphasize individual experience include that of William James, (1842-1910) "Religion means the feelings, acts, and experiences of individual men in their solitude, so far as they apprehend themselves to stand in relation to whatever they may consider divine."

Carl Jung (1875-1961) defines religion as, “the attitude peculiar to a consciousness which has been changed by experience of the numinosum.” Examples of individually oriented religious experience also include shamans and mystics.

Edward Conze (1904-79) offers a meditative definition. “A religion is an organization of spiritual aspirations, which reject the sensory world and negate the impulses which bind us to it.” This definition by Conze, a Buddhist scholar, pertains to the highly cognitive psychological-philosophical orientation of Theravada Buddhism. For existentialist theologian Paul Tillich, (1886-1965) religion consists of an individual’s “ultimate concern...which itself contains the answer to the question of the meaning of life” (McDermott, 1999).

For Melford Spiro, (1920) religion is a social “institution of culturally patterned interaction with culturally postulated superhuman beings,” and since these beings are postulated, they may or may not actually exist. Social-ethical definitions include the biblical view, “Pure religion and undefiled before God and the Father is this, to visit the fatherless and the widows in their affliction, and to keep himself unspotted from the world” (James, 1:27). Matthew Arnold (1822-88) thinks that, “Religion is ethics heightened, enkindled, lit up by feeling.” However, these mainly monotheistic ethical definitions of religion emerged only much later in human development and population growth. With an increase of population and the eventual development of social classes came political definitions such as those advocated by Karl Marx (1818-83). “Religion is the sigh of the oppressed creature, the heart of a heartless world, and the soul of soulless conditions. It is the opium of the people.” For Marx religion assists people, especially the proletariat or workers, to feel better about their condition of poverty in a class struggle for the material goods of society. Early scholarly definitions include those of James Frazer, (1894-1941) who defined religion as “the propitiation or conciliation of powers superior to man which are believed to direct and control the course of Nature and human life,” and Friedrich Schleiermacher (1768-1834) for whom “The essence of religion consists in the feeling of an absolute dependence” (McDermott, 1999).

But not all religions seek to appease or gain the good will of a superior presence in the form of a personal god, for example, the impersonal Tao in China or Brahman in Hinduism; nor are humans always completely dependent upon their deities. Many deities are in vogue for a time and are then as a result of social changes replaced; for example, in modern Iran the earlier Zoroastrian deity Ahura Mazda has been superseded by the Muslim deity Allah. The following quote expresses pessimism toward the dynamic of religion and change.

"The religions of man each prevail,
Until one comes to triumph and the other fail;
Ah, the lonesome world;
Always wants to hear the latest fairy tale." (Al Ma'arri, 973-1058)

Historic expressions and definitions of religion can be limited to an individual or group practice; to a concern with ethics as a determination of what is right or wrong and good or evil; or to an emphasis on morals as the customs and rules by which humans live, that eventually became a basis for a political/legal system. Religion can also consist of varying practices such as the use of certain symbols and gatherings for the performance of ritual behaviors such as remaining silent, listening to sermons, singing, or prostration that have been observed and studied and then used by scholars to define religion.

There is a wide and varying range of limited definitions of the term religion. Each of these definitions is limited to a particular time, geographical location, cultural tradition, or discipline. I have reviewed many definitions of the word religion so as to discern a basic or essential meaning that would apply to religion, regardless of time, place, or tradition. This essential definition can serve as a basis to better comprehend the artifact evidence from three areas during the Paleolithic era that suggest the presence of what could be the earliest and longest-lasting religious view of humankind and its eventual decline.

In the search for a definitional essence of the word religion, it would be prudent to consider the etymology of the term and to find how and in what context it was originally used. The Roman orator Cicero (106-43 BCE) traced the word religion to the Latin word *relegere*. According to Cicero, the Romans of his time were called religious or *relegere* because they recalled from memory and repeated whatever pertained to the worship of the deities. This might have been what occurred when the Romans gathered or assembled in relationship to a deity, but what was the intention for this expressive behavior? Muller agrees with Cicero's claim about the origin of the word and considers it originally and primarily to have meant "to look back," and remarks that various secondary meanings can be understood to include to retrace, to find one's way back, and to connect together (Muller, 1882, p. 11).

After the time of Tertullian during the third century, Christian scholars considered the word religion to be derived from the Latin *religare* "to bind together."Ries (1994) sees the Christian meaning given to the word religion as the binding of humans to God through the teaching and rituals begun by the early group leaders of the church (p. 7). This view is supported by Laetantius, an early church leader who thought that piety was a bond through which humans were bound and tied to God and from which religion gets the name (Ducasse, 1953, p. 94). St. Augustine also derived the word religion from *religare*, taking it to mean to bind, or to fasten (Muller, 1882, p. 12).

According to the etymology and earliest use of the term by the Romans and later Christians in Rome, religion implies to find one's way back, to reconnect. For this study, the term religion is defined as meaning, "to find one's way back to the beginning and to reconnect to the origin of life and the environment." The primary intention of religion has been and is to identify or make known the unknown beginning of living forms and the environment.

This is an essentialist and functional definition, as it seeks to define the essence and function of religion. Thus, the essence of all religions is to make the unknown beginning of environment and life known.

This attention to beginnings was usually not directed to cause-and-effect processes of the environment and mental processes within, but rather to the supernatural or to what was beyond or exceeded the natural.

Feuerbach (1957) says that in religion attention is directed to "the first, the supreme being" (p. 12), in other words, the beginning. By means of religion, humans have always sought to know from where or what all things, including themselves, have come in the past, from where or what events come in the present, and to what or where will all things go at the time of physical death in the future. Throughout recorded human existence there have been a great many identifications of the beginning of existence. My definition of religion applies to all variations of its expression including animistic, pantheistic, polytheistic, and theistic, as well as to the non-theistic philosophical religions.

For example, in the animistic religion of the Andamanese, a basic or an indigenous group inhabiting an archipelago in the Bay of Bengal, the northwest monsoon is considered to be a female named Biliku, who is the mate of Tarai, the male southwest monsoon. Their children are the sun, the moon, and the birds, and from a union of the sun and moon came forth the stars. Biliku made the first man, Tomo, and eventually Lady Crab, the first woman (Campbell, 1987, pp. 367-368). In the pantheistic religion of the Sioux Indians of North America, at the very beginning of existence there was a primal rock upon which an elk suddenly appeared and began to bellow loudly. In response to this event the Sioux explain that the first dawn appeared from the darkness of the space surrounding the rock, and that the rock, dark space, elk, and dawn, and later other forms including humans, are all parts of Wakantaka, the Supreme Spirit (Eliot, 1976, p. 62).

The polytheistic Greek religion traced the beginning of existence to chaos, a vast expanse from which appeared Gaia, the female earth, who gave birth to Uranos, the male sky. From their joining the many Greek deities and also eventually humans and all other things came into existence.

In the theistic Hebrew Genesis story, the beginning of existence, including both good and evil and humans who chose to have knowledge, is traced to the spoken words of the combined deities Yahweh-Elohim, usually translated into English as the Lord God.

For later Christians, the beginning of good, as well as an afterlife existence, came from Abba or the Father, and when one died, one's spirit joined the presence of the deity in heaven. In that tradition, evil came into existence from a former angel variously known as Lucifer, the Devil, or Satan. A Hindu story identifies the beginning or origin of sapphires as having come from a tear of the creator god Brahma (Molyneaux, 1995, p. 83).

In the non-theistic Theravada Buddhist tradition, the beginning of existence was traced to avidya or ignorance and karma within oneself as desires and volitions. Reducing ignorance and karma resulted in the calm of Nirvana and the cessation of rebirth. In Taoism the beginning was found in the Tao or chi, the primordial energy from which came the complimentary opposites of Yin-Yang.

These examples provide evidence for my contention that the basic or essential meaning of religion consists of an individual and/or group intention to find one's way back to the beginning, and to reconnect to the origin of life and the environment. I will seek to establish that this primary intention for the phenomenon of religion, to identify or make known the unknown beginning of life, first developed through innate cognitive processes during the Paleolithic era circa 100,000 BP.

Cognitive Processes and the Origin of Religion

Since religion has been defined as the intention to identify or to make known the unknown beginning of life and the environment, then a discussion of how this was accomplished by Paleolithic peoples is necessary. In this endeavor, I will evaluate the human cognitive processes which must be considered (Marshack, 1991, p. 340) in order to fully comprehend the origin of religion.

When discussing the origin of religion, researchers usually fail to adequately discuss human cognitive processes as a precursor of behavior. What follows is an in-depth investigation of the phenomena of cognitive processes that contributed to the earliest development of religion, and a critique of how previous theories for religion have neglected to discuss these important mental functions.

Four innate cognitive processes have contributed to identifying the origin of living forms. These are the mental processes of animism, anthropomorphism, dreams, a use of rudimentary analogical reasoning, and the two general cognitive orientations of gynocentrism and geocentrism.

Tylor (1958) thought that religion began when early humans observed and pondered about what makes the difference between a living body and a dead one. They also wondered about the images of deceased humans that appeared in visions and dreams (p. 12). Humans through rudimentary reasoning, conceived the view that the body contained an "anima" or spirit that survived physical death. The presence of a spirit was attributed to humans, to animals, and to formations of the environment such as the wind, water, storms, and so on. For Tylor, the origin of religion from ancient to modern times is found in what he calls "animism," the belief in spiritual beings (p. 8). Early peoples attributed, not only to humans, but also to animals and inanimate objects, a conceived "phantom...a thin unsubstantial...vapour, film, or shadow; the cause of life and thought in the individual...independently possessing...personal consciousness and volition...capable of leaving the body." Today we would call this a spirit or soul (pp. 12-13).

Tylor's evidence for the origin and development of religion is based on studying many of the historical cultures that he visited in North Africa and Mexico. My disagreement with Tylor's view is twofold. First, I disagree with his definition of animism as the belief in spirits; modern psychology has a more relevant definition which will be discussed. Secondly, Tylor's view of a belief in spirits by early humans is based on his use of analogy and comparison with historic contemporary tribal cultures, which from a phenomenological point of view is limiting, unreliable, and unacceptable.

My view of the origin of religion is based on a better comprehension and definition of the term animism that is supported by modern psychology. More than likely, early or prehistoric peoples attributed the processes of the environment to an animated entity having intentions or thoughts.

Not having notions of cause and effect to explain the motion or function of natural processes, humans used what they were most familiar with in their own evolving awareness. The movement of flowing water, storms, sun, moon, and planets were likely understood as being alive and as having conscious intentions or thought. For early humans, any natural phenomenon that moved was more accurately perceived as an animated entity capable of thinking, rather than as possessing a metaphysical spirit or soul.

Modern psychology provides a more relevant definition of animism as the "attribution of life to nonliving forms." Animism is an innate or early developed cognitive function of the perceptual system that is oriented to changes in motion and the relationships of changes in motion. The human brain/mind interprets these changes as caused by internal or external factors. Concepts of aliveness, intent, and purpose are based upon this primitive biological function (Travers, 1996). For Paleolithic humans, the movement of a comet, an avalanche, or a thunderstorm probably derived from an intentional, living entity.

Early human experience that life only comes from life and not from what was dead or unmoving, and the observation of plants and trees growing from the soil and insects and animals entering and exiting holes and dens probably resulted in the animistic view that the earth was alive. While I agree with Tylor that animism is a contributing factor to the origin of religion, I disagree with him when he insists that prehistoric humans attributed a "spirit or soul" to animate and inanimate forms. Instead, early humans more than likely would have perceived moving processes as living and then projected onto them the mental processes of intentions and thoughts. This cognitive process is usually known as anthropomorphism.

Muller (1882) claimed that religion is a mental ability or disposition that enables humans to apprehend the infinite, using different names and under varying forms. All religions, including the worship of idols and fetishes, are a struggle to understand the unknown, to speak the unspeakable. Religion is a longing after the infinite (pp.22- 23). These characteristics point to the second main cognitive process that has contributed to the origin of religion, anthropomorphism.

The origin of existence usually has human characteristics. The divine being is nothing else than the human being...the human nature...freed from the limits of the individual...made objective...contemplated and revered as another, a distinct being. All the attributes of the divine nature are, therefore, attributes of the human nature (Feuerbach, 1957, p. 14).

In early times, to recognize the origin of life, humans projected personal qualities such as intentions, caring, love, and protection onto visible forms, or in later times to unseen abstract entities. An entity lacking attributes is one that cannot become an object of attention (p. 14). Humans projected an entity having human attributes that made the environment and living forms, including themselves.

While I agree with Feuerbach on the cognitive function of anthropomorphism in humans as contributing to the origin and development of religion, I disagree with him on the mechanism for how this comes about. For Feuerbach, religion is merely a primitive, childish, popular, prejudiced, and un-emancipated view of the human self and nature (p. 116). In other words, anthropomorphism is a result of an evolving yet cognitive immaturity that is confirmed by the group and prejudiced in favor of humans over other human groups or sentient species. Religion is also the experience of mental and physical personal limitation in the environment.

I find more agreement with Gutherie's (1993) definition of anthropomorphism. He defines anthropomorphism as the attribution of human qualities to nonhuman things or events (p. 3) that occurs as a result of perception which is a spontaneous and unconscious interpretive tendency to find significance or meaning (p. 7).

Perception is an innate function of survival whereby humans find themselves in a dubious and ambiguous world. Thus, they use themselves as a model with which to interpret it (p. 38). Gutherie has surveyed developmental, clinical, and experimental studies of children and adults and concludes that a generalized anthropomorphism is spontaneous in both children and adults (p. 121). He disagrees with views that see anthropomorphism as irrational, the result of confusion or wishful thinking. Rather, he sees the strong tendency for anthropomorphism as the most powerful innate biological and cognitive human strategy to identify and understand the unknown cause of things or events through use of the human self as analogy (pp. 69-70).

Gutherie produces many convincing visual and literary examples of the pervasive presence of anthropomorphism from early and contemporary art, literature, advertising, philosophy, and even science. He sums up his survey with the following statement:

"Although philosophers and scientists are the people wariest of anthropomorphism, and although most now regard it as unalloyed error, they are as prone to it as the rest of us. And while modern reflection tends to diminish it, some forms, generally judged inoffensive, survive. Anthropomorphism, then, though fundamental neither to philosophy nor to science, criticized by both and evidently antithetical at least to science, continues to appear in them. If we find it in the margins even of these enterprises, in religion, from which it appears inextricable, we should not be surprised to find it at the center" (p. 176).

I agree that religion originates in subconscious perception using human attributes. There can be no communication or prayer to a non-anthropomorphic deity. In other words, a deity that has no human likeness in form and/or thoughts is not meaningful. Making the unknown beginning of things and events known is an attempt to find meaning.

The English word "meaning" is traced to the German word *meinen*, defined as "to have in the mind as a purpose or intention directed to a particular object." This definition implies a subject-object or relative sensory or imagined relationship. The meaning of a thing is tied or associated with attention or awareness. What is unknown would be meaningless, since there is no relative relationship.

Recent studies suggest that the cognitive tendency to anthropomorphism is innate. Research with newborn and older infants has found that sub-cortical or innate mechanisms predispose newborns to look toward a human face rather than other stimuli. Also, results measured at 6-and 12-week intervals suggest an increase in cortical influence over infant preference to respond to the human face (Mondloch et al., 1999). This study shows an innate predisposition to seek and cognize human features in the environment that could contribute to the later perceptual mechanism of anthropomorphism found by Gutherie to be present in young children and adults.

Sigmund Freud (1961) defined religion as a psychological delusion, a mistaken idea. For Freud, the shared task of humanity is to safeguard itself against nature. The phenomena of both a cooperative civilization and religious views have originated from the individual need to defend against the superior forces of nature (p. 21). This is done by humanizing nature, since impersonal forces cannot be communicated with by humans (p. 16). By attributing a volition or will to the forces of nature, humans seek to influence them. This cognitive process originates in the phylogenetic and individual helplessness of childhood that gives to these forces the character of a father (p. 17).

Freud also thought that in satisfying the child's hunger, the mother becomes the first love-object and protection from danger and anxiety. The mother's protection is later replaced by the physically stronger father's. Thereafter, the father retains that position. Individual helplessness for the child and for the adult, becomes the motive of longing or desire for protection that contributes to the formation of a religion (p. 24).

Having a god, then, is a wish-fulfilling illusion or delusion (p. 31). For Freud religion has its beginnings in emotion, phylogenetic instinct, and subconscious childhood memories. Religion is not the result of intelligent conscious reasoning processes, but is the cognitive distortion of a subconscious obsessional neurosis (p. 46).

In contrast, my view of the cognitive origin and development of religion is based on the earliest use and meaning of the word, which is to reconnect with and to make the unknown origin of life and the environment known. Religion is not the projection of a cognitive distortion or neurosis; rather it is a cognitive strategy to determine the beginning or origin of existence.

I do agree with Freud that forces of the environment have been humanized or anthropomorphized. While Freud implies the cognitive function of animism, of attributing life to non-living forms, he does not specifically mention it in his view as I have done. I also agree with Freud that anthropomorphism is a subconscious cognitive process that aids in human survival strategy, and yet that it is a mistaken idea. While humans can anthropomorphically obsess about the origin of existence, I would not consider this to be a neurosis or cognitive dysfunction, but rather a way of surviving the difficulties of existence.

Freud attributes the mechanism of anthropomorphism to phylogenetic instinct, which I understand to be innate. I am willing to accept Freud's view of anthropomorphism as an innate cognitive process, and I also accept that the subconscious memories of childhood may contribute to the phenomenon of anthropomorphism and the beginning of religion. However, a main point of contention between my view of the beginning of religion and that of Freud is that he insists that the mother is the primary care-giver and protector and that this role is replaced by the father during early childhood. As a consequence humans anthropomorphize the origin of existence as male.

I will present artifact evidence that strongly supports the view that during the Middle and Upper Paleolithic eras, circa 100,000-10,000 BP, the origin of existence was exclusively and gynocentrically perceived as the mother. Even though the male presence was required for protection and hunting, the evidence confirms that the origin of life was not associated with the male until circa 10,000 BP.

A final difference between Freud's theory and mine is that while he thought that religion began in genetic instinct and the subconscious memory and emotions of fear and helplessness experienced during childhood, he did not think that conscious reasoning played a part. I argue that rudimentary reasoning using analogy, comparing "this with that," is a cognitive process that has also contributed to the origin and development of the earliest religion.

Mircea Eliade (1969) was primarily an historian and secondarily a phenomenologist of religion who defined the word religion as that which refers to an "experience of the sacred" (p. i). The sacred is a discovery made by the human mind. This orientation can be found in the distinction made between the sacred and the profane. In the practice of religion, there are sacred things and also sacred times, as well as profane things and profane times. Sacred things are associated with the beginning, whereas profane things are not. Sacred things are distinguished by a hierophany, meaning what is sacred shows itself to humans (1959, p. 10).

The sacred object, whether it be a stone or a tree, has been consecrated or has been made sacred by humans, as it contained and/or expressed a power to bring forth a certain effect (p. 12). Eliade thought that the defining characteristic of religion is that humans have a nostalgia for the perfection of the time of the beginning. The religious person expresses a difficult to satisfy ontological thirst for what is ultimately real, which is the time of the beginning that gave meaning to the everyday profane changes of daily life (p. 92).

I agree with Eliade's view that religion usually involves making a distinction between sacred and profane places, both in the environment and in time, as a means of locating the beginning of things and events. I also agree that myths and rituals are a way of returning to and so experiencing the sacred time of the beginning (pp. 80, 104). However, Eliade's view lacks discussion of how the consecration of a sacred place or object occurs.

For Eliade, determining what is sacred and what is profane or every day is a dialectical process of conscious reasoning and questioning of the ontological status of objects, and then classifying them as either sacred or profane. Human choice singles out a particular object or process from others. What is out of the ordinary, large, or novel is usually regarded as a hierophany or manifestation of the sacred (1963, pp. 13, 26). Eliade also argues that the sacred is a structure within consciousness, (Eliade, 1969, p. i) but he does not discuss or explain how this occurs. Attributing an ontological thirst to humans seems to be merely a way of saying that humans have an innate desire or curiosity. By contrast, my definition clearly defines and discusses the cognitive processes of how religion came into existence through animism, anthropomorphism, dreaming, and rudimentary reasoning.

Durkheim (1965) sociologically defines religion as an organized system of beliefs and practices relative to sacred things. He claims it sets apart and/or forbids beliefs and practices whose acceptance serves to unite into one moral community, a church (p. 62). Religion begins with an emotional effervescence (p. 422) during a ritual and leads to the cognitive process of idealization (p. 469).

This cognitive process contributes to identifying and determining what is sacred, namely, what is added to and above the actual world that differs from the profane or everyday life. Religion comes from collective conceptions that become the basic elements of religion and gradually become agreed upon sentiments among the individual members of the group (p. 463). Religion is also a cosmology, a rational grouping of ideas that correspond to a particular object varying from religion to religion (pp. 463, 466).

Society is the guardian, support, and refuge of the individual (p. 465). Collective society is the "objective cause" of the individual and constructs the religious experience of ritual behaviors. The individual conscience is formed from the group (p. 472). As a result of group living, society develops morals: the customs and the rules by which humans live. Based on these characteristics, Durkheim thought that a deity was an idealized symbol of society.

I disagree with Durkheim's interpretation. While this description may be the way a group religion functions, it is not the basic or essential intention for a religion. Nor would I agree that religion is a complete rational system of conscious ideas or concepts. There is more to the cognitive process of locating the sacred beginning of events or existence. Conscious emotional idealization of objects, conceptualization, and sentiment are not adequate to explain the beginning of religion.

Clark (1977) contradicts Durkheim's view on the definition and origin of religion, defining religion as beginning within the personal experience of the individual when he or she senses the beyond (p. 769). Clark does not identify the beginning of religion with group dynamics, but with individual mystical experience. He cites as examples ethnobotanical or drug induced altered states of consciousness, mediumship or shamanism, anecdotal reports of disembodied spirits and hauntings, the siddhis or paranormal abilities of yoga, and events in the Bible such as healing and survival after death. This cognitive sensing of the beyond occurs in the nonrational processes of the subconscious mind, including intuition, and is made sensible by conscious reasoning.

I agree with Clark that the attention of religion is usually directed to what is beyond the ordinary to visible or invisible forms or to non-ordinary abilities associated with the beginning of existence and events.

While it is not possible to deny that mystical or paranormal experience is part of religion, especially as found in the practices of historical shamanism, there is no evidence of this during the Paleolithic era, although some researchers (Eliade, 1978; Lewis-Williams & Dowson, 1988; Clottes & Lewis-Williams, 1998) have attempted to advance this view. My investigation of Paleolithic era artifacts suggest these finds are remnant evidence of the perceptual processes of animism, anthropomorphism, and dreams.

The phenomenon of dreaming is another innate subconscious perceptual process that has contributed to finding the origin of human existence. As previously mentioned, Tylor (1958) thought that early historic tribal humans were perplexed by two biological problems. First, what makes the difference between a dead body and a living body? Second, what were those human shapes that often appeared in dreams (p. 12)? He says that early humans thought that these images were the phantom, ghost, spirit, or animating soul of deceased relatives and friends, and even animals. Tylor thought this experience contributed to the origin and development of early religion, yet his argument is based on what is known of historic cultures. What Paleolithic era humans thought of this phenomenon may remain unknown.

However, it may be more rewarding to rephrase Tylor's question of what early humans asked themselves. More precisely, as there is the artifact evidence of burial to support this view, Paleolithic humans asked "where" were the human images located that appeared in dreams.

Like animism and anthropomorphism, dreams are a subconscious cognitive function that prehistoric peoples would have had in common with modern humans. Dreams occur nightly without conscious intention, nor can dreams be prevented. Humans have a continuum of mental function ranging from focused conscious attention and thought to imagination and to dreaming, all of which occur in the cerebral cortex (Hartmann, 1999, pp. 64-66).

The phenomenon of sleep makes up one-third of human existence. It is known that the two main stages of the sleep state are alternating cycles of rapid eye movement (REM) and non-rapid eye movement (NREM). Researchers agree that the mental activity of dreaming takes place in the cerebral cortex and occurs during all stages of sleep, especially during REM sleep. During the alternating REM sleep stages that total approximately two hours nightly, the brain is as active as when awake. Examining an electroencephalogram of both sleep stages, one would have difficulty distinguishing between waking and dreaming (Bulkeley, 1997, p. 56).

Since most mammals have been observed to experience REM sleep, which is strongly associated with vivid dreaming, sleep laboratory researchers have concluded that dreams probably had some evolutionary value. Research results suggest that dreams function to process experiences that occurred during waking hours. "Dreaming serves to promote the general adaptation of people to their environment, helping them to organize their perceptions...and to connect and integrate new experiences with past memories" (Bulkeley, 1997, pp. 65, 84). Whether dream images are the result of wish fulfillment, existential situations, precognition, or just the random residue of daytime events, it may be safely assumed that the phenomenon would have been of interest to early humans during the gradually evolving increase of cognitive abilities.

Geist (1978) speculates that the intention in Neanderthal burial emerged from dream images of the deceased. Living in small groups, each individual would have been important for group survival. The loss of a group member would have been an especially poignant and traumatic experience. Seeing images of the deceased in dreams could have contributed to care given to the body after death (p. 320).

While also speculative, my view is that the relationship of dreams with darkness also possibly contributed to the intention for early human burials under the surface of the earth and in caves. Early humans' dreams could have functioned as a "paraworld" (States, 1997, p. 67) that provided a context in which the dead could interact with the living.

If dreams came during the night, where was it always night? The phenomena of sleep and death appear similar; and since humans slept during darkness, then the dead body was placed where it was dark. Early humans could also have thought the images of deceased humans came from or were located within the darkness of the earth interior.

Geertz (1973) does not think the subconscious perceptual processes of animism, anthropomorphism, and dreams are important in the development of religion. Instead, he thinks the human mind consciously seeks and gathers information through experience of the external world in order to determine the emotional importance of events. This serves to motivate, inform, or shape the reasoning of conceptual thinking and results in the meaningful shared symbols of a deity, ritual, myth, or art (pp. 81-83). He defines religion as a system of symbols which acts to establish powerful, pervasive, and long-lasting moods and motivations in humans by formulating conceptions of a general order of existence, and clothing these conceptions with such an aura of factuality that the moods and motivations seem uniquely realistic (p. 90).

Geertz defines a symbol as any form, action, event, quality, or relationship that serves as an object for conception and meaning (p. 91). Conceived symbols, he says, are a response to experienced and unexpected trauma, suffering, evil, and loss in what at times seems an absurd existence (pp. 102-105). The symbols of religion direct human attention away from this existence to a greater dimension indicated through the use of religious symbolism by denying that these irrationalities exist (p. 108). Religious views, including those of goddesses, gods, demons, and spirits, have been developed by reason to provide an answer to the problem of meaning when humans experience uncertainty, suffering, moral confusion, and meaninglessness (p. 109). Religion gives meaning to existence through the use of reason and conceptions that contribute to individual understanding and social order.

I agree with Renfrew's (1994) criticism when he comments that, by avoiding mention of the supernatural or sacred in his definition of religion, Geertz's view is so lacking in focus that it could apply to secular ritual or even to the system of values which is used to uphold a monetary economy. Such a definition lacks any sense of what must surely be a component of any religion, the individual religious experience (p. 48).

Geertz's view ignores the cognitive antecedent and basis for conception, which is perception. In order to relate to an origin, humans would have first to perceive or identify what is there, which would be the result of innate and mostly subconscious animistic and anthropomorphic perception. Only after having a basic perceptual awareness could conscious reasoning develop concepts and use symbols. Other researchers such as Moustakas (1994) rightly think that, during the process of knowing, there is a constant flow of both perceiving and conceptualizing (p. 80). While perception is the primary and dominant aspect of this process, conceptual reasoning through use of analogy also plays a role in the origin of religion.

Reasoning by analogy consists of an association of relating "this with that." Imitation in tool making by Homo erectus, Neanderthals, and Homo sapiens sapiens, suggest that early humans possessed an ability to recognize similarity. Neanderthals used 63 types of flake tools (Chase & Dibble, 1987, p. 271). This ability would have necessitated a learned set of purposeful behaviors and planning and a talent for imitation, making one tool like another (Klein, 1990). This could indicate a developing ability for rudimentary analogical reasoning as well.

Horton & Finnegan (1973) point out that, in the use of magical thinking by historical tribal groups, the use of analogy serves three distinct functions.

"An object may be named or described by referring to another object which it resembles...the recognition of a resemblance between two objects may serve as the basis for an explanation of one of them...the resemblances between things may be thought to form magical links between them and attempts may be made to control or influence certain objects by manipulating other objects which resemble them" (p. 206).

Whether in magic or science, the use of analogy serves to provide an explanation and to predict. Caution has been urged in the use of analogical reasoning in modern science and computer programs as similarities are prone not be accurate and are often misleading. If verification-based, however, the use of analogy can at least stimulate creative thought (Mishra, 1998).

It is evident that the use of analogy has also contributed to the origin of religion in the written record of humankind (Horton & Finnegan, 1973). Analogy has contributed to human explanations of the world, how it was created, and why events unfold as they do. Many different cultures have found it natural to explain puzzling aspects of the world by talking of gods who created the world and influence it in various ways. Despite their enhanced powers, these gods are in many important respects often remarkably similar to people. The reason is simple: people create gods in their own image (p. 167). Along with the cognitive processes of animism, anthropomorphism, and dreams, evidence suggests that rudimentary reasoning using analogy also influenced the development of the first religion.

A number of researchers argue that the cognitive orientation of gynocentrism has contributed to the origin of religion. For Murray, (1963) every religion is the expression of the effort to solve the mystery of existence, of how it began and how it eventually ends (p. 7). She thinks the phenomenon of religion began in the evolving Paleolithic female mind (p. 1) with the startling yet simple and mysterious physical experiences of quickening, giving birth, and nurturing (pp. 62, 67-69).

Prior to knowledge of the male contribution to reproduction, the female was perceived to be the sole cause of the newborn. She was the life-giver and the exclusive food-giver; yet how this process occurred was unknown to her. Knowledge of the male contribution to reproduction only occurred during the beginning of agriculture when men no longer hunted and began to spend more time in settled communities with women (pp. 4-8).

For Paleolithic peoples, it is likely that child-bearing began at a very early age (p. 66). From her study of historical cultures, Murray concludes it was quite common that a young girl became a wife as early as her first menstruation, a mother at 11 or 12, and a grandmother by the age of 25 (p. 81). During the advanced stage of pregnancy and reduced activity, the condition of pregnancy occupied much of the expectant mother's thoughts. A group of pregnant women having the capacity of speech would have discussed their experiences of quickening and carrying the fetus. They would have anticipated the pending event of childbirth, perhaps considering it to be an awesome as well as a painful and dangerous event. Therefore, they postulated various views about this phenomenon (p. 68).

Murray thinks Paleolithic women would have thought that the moving fetus within them was placed there by an unseen deity namely, the "goddess of pregnancy" to whom women would have turned in the months of waiting (p. 68). She argues that the Venus figures represent a goddess of pregnancy, developed as an explanation of the origin of the moving presence of life within the womb and who could be looked to for protection and comfort during the ordeal of pregnancy and birthing.

Like Geertz's, Murray's view is a rationalist explanation for the origin of religion. She thinks that the earliest religion was developed by conscious reasoning processes in women. I disagree with her for the same reasons I disagree with Geertz's view. The origin of religion consisted of more than the conscious conceptual process of reasoning; it included the subconscious perceptual functions of animism, anthropomorphism, and dreams.

In my view, the Venus or female figures represent, not a goddess of childbirth, but an anthropomorphism of the earth as the greater origin of living forms. I do agree with Murray that characteristics associated with women, such as bringing forth life, contributed to a dominant gynocentric orientation during the development of the first religion.

In this section I have discussed the innate cognitive processes that have contributed to the development of a religious view and how other theories of religion have failed to adequately comprehend and explain these functions. In the following section I will examine the artifacts from the Middle and Upper Paleolithic era circa 100,000-10,000 BP for evidence of a religious view and practice during this time.

Evidence for Religion During the Paleolithic

Based upon my definition of religion as the intention to identify or make known the unknown beginning of living forms and the environment, there is artifact evidence from three areas that a religious view developed during the Paleolithic era circa 100,000 BP, and continued until 10,000 BP. These areas of evidence for a religious view include Neanderthal burial, Paleolithic cave art, and female figurines.

Many views exist in regard to human burials that first began with Neanderthals circa 100,000 BP and continued until their extinction circa 30,000 BP. Gargett (1989) argues that the burials were not intentional, while Kooijmans, et al. (1989) argues the burials were intentional. If researchers accept the view that the remains were intentionally buried, theories vary as to the intention, emotional bonds, (Chase & Dibble, 1987) hygiene, (Tattersall, 1995; Stringer & Gamble, 1993) and others.

I will argue that Neanderthals did intentionally bury the dead and that this behavior is the result of a geocentric religious view. Interring the human body in the soil of rock-shelters and caves reveals a meaningful interaction with the earth and a religious view that the beginning of life came from within the earth.

Having a brain similar to modern humans, Neanderthals very likely had the innate cognitive capacity for three mostly subconscious in addition to conscious mental processes. The first is animism, defined psychologically as attributing life to non-living things. The second process is anthropomorphism, the mostly subconscious attribution of human characteristics to nonhuman things or processes. The third occurs during sleep with the vivid imagery of dreams. Neanderthals, based on the artifact evidence of imitation in tool making, were also capable of rudimentary analogical reasoning; they reasoned "this is like that."

When Neanderthals experienced helplessness after a death occurred, what could they do? The living could not bring the deceased back to life, regardless of what they might do to the body. One possibility could have been to place the individual back into the female human body from which it had its origin, restoring life and giving birth to the deceased again. However, this was not possible. The only emotionally effective behavior was to protectively place the lifeless form where most of life originated, the interior of the earth which was most easily accessed by entering rock-shelters and caves. Through the innate psychological processes of animism, anthropomorphism, dreams, and rudimentary analogical reasoning, humans perceived and conceived the earth to be the origin of life and existence. In my view, burial was the rudimentary expression of a religious view.

Evidence of this religious view, that the interior of the earth was the origin of life, continues with Homo sapiens sapiens who also buried the dead, and the phenomenon of European cave art circa 35,000-10,000 BP.

Many theories seek to explain the existence of Paleolithic cave or parietal art, defined as images engraved, drawn, painted, or sculpted on the ceilings, walls and floors of caves. Most prevalent are the androcentric views that consider it to be an expression of male hunting or fertility magic, (Breuil, 1979) and shamanistic rituals (Lewis-Williams & Dowson, 1988).

I argue there is evidence that suggests the images of animals and hand prints were drawn primarily but not exclusively by women. This artistic behavior was a result of the perceptual processes of animism, anthropomorphism, dream imagery, and the analogically reasoned and conceptual gynocentric view of the interior of the earth as the female origin of existence. The engraved and painted images were a "petition" by artist "midwives" who assisted the earth to bring forth life.

Support for this view is found in the findings and statements of Paleolithic field researchers knowledgeable in the area of the physical dimensions of Paleolithic humans, (Leroi-Gourhan, 1967, p. 477) and the size of artifact hand prints and footprints left by the artists in numerous caves, especially the Gargas and Pech-Merle sites in France. This "petitionary-midwife" model also explains an anomaly in the faunal record for which few convincing previous explanations have been offered. This anomaly is the discrepancy between the species of animals portrayed in the cave art, and the faunal remains of animals eaten by the inhabitants.

The third and further evidence for a religious view developing during the Paleolithic includes the sculpted female figures produced from circa 30,000-12,000 BP. Theories about these female images include the view that they functioned as figures to increase or glorify human fertility and reproduction, (Giedon, 1962) to an honoring of womanhood, (Rice, 1982) or that they represent a medical condition of enlarged breast development (Harding, 1976).

The female figures have few facial features, the feet are missing and the hands are usually not present. While present on the Willendorf Venus and only a few others, vulvae are missing from the majority of the female images. Nipples are not on the breasts, and the figures are never portrayed in childbirth, nursing, or with children. There is little evidence of clothing. These figures do not represent an accurate and natural image of the human female. Lacking these details, which the artists were capable of portraying, the female figures appear to be generalized images, not a particular identifiable human being.

I will argue that these female figurines are not Venus figures; instead they are "Earth figures," and are the earliest anthropomorphic representation of a deity, the earth and especially its interior as the female origin of existence. The unknown shape of the earth was given form through the cognitive process of anthropomorphism. The figures are a perceived and conceived gynocentric and geocentric combination of the knowledge of where living forms came from: the female human body and the mysterious interior of the earth.

In my view, religion began during Paleolithic times when humans first began to identify the origin of life. Locating the beginning of existence within the earth resulted in the burying of the body. Cave art with its engravings and paintings was an expression of the concern for locating the beginning of animal and plant life. The female figures represent an anthropomorphism of the greater origin of life, the earth. The three areas of Neanderthal burials, cave art, and female figures are conjoined by a singly developed and long lasting geocentric and gynocentric religious view that the beginning of life came from within the earth.

Paleolithic humans were geocentric; much of their daily attention was centered on the earth, especially the interior of the earth that provided the nourishment of plants that grew from within and the insects and animals born and living inside its crevices, burrows, and dens. Paleolithic humans were also gynocentric, attention was predominantly centered on women. Life came from her body and she was the provider of the nourishment and care essential for survival during infancy. In Middle and Upper Paleolithic times, at least some of the tribal members would have been present during the birth process and would have experienced wonder and awe at the ability of the female to bring forth life from within her body.

The young woman would have crouched or lain upon the earth during the process of giving birth and would have been observed and perceived as doing what the earth does: bringing forth life from within. Through thousands of years a strong subconscious perception and consciously conceived association was then formed that the earth was like the human female; it also brought forth life from within.

In conclusion, the basic or intentional essence and function of a religion is that it identifies or makes known the origin of living forms and the environment. This was accomplished during the Paleolithic era through the innate subconscious perceptual processes of animism, anthropomorphism, and dreams and through the conscious conceptual reasoning of analogy.

These cognitive processes, along with a gynocentric and geocentric orientation, all contributed to the origin of the first and longest-lasting religion of humankind as evidenced in the artifacts of Neanderthal burial, cave art, and the female figures.

Chapter 2

Use of Analogy by Researchers

The evidence for the earliest developed and longest-enduring religious idea and practice, is found in the expressions of Neanderthal burial, cave art, and female figures dating from circa 100,000-10,000 BP. In seeking evidence of a Paleolithic religious view, I have researched these three phenomena as presented in the scholarly literature of journal articles and books, and made field trips to museums and to France to study Paleolithic artifacts. I examined archeological remains, journal articles, and books for reliable knowledge of the artifacts. Having investigated the remnant artifacts and the various theories, I contend these three phenomena convincingly support the assertion that there did exist a religious view and practice during Middle and Upper Paleolithic times.

In my discussions of the evidence, analogical reasoning is kept to a minimum. The dictionary defines the term analogy as an "inference that if two or more things agree with one another in some respects they will probably agree in others." Essentially the use of analogy consists of a reasoning process that infers that X is like X, and if X has quality Y, then X will probably have quality Y also. The question is whether X is so much like X that it is convincing to expect other qualities to be similar. This key premise is usually unstated, and even when made explicit it is typically weak and in need of further defense. The use of analogy in the discipline of philosophy is considered to be a fallacy of relevance.

Lewis-Williams (1991) comments on the problem of using analogy, especially as it pertains to Paleolithic era research (p. 149). He first presents an example of the use of analogy and the erroneous results obtained from doing so in past European cave art research, and observes that in this instance the researcher's use of analogy was based on only three shared similarities.

Lewis-Williams suggests that when using analogical reasoning the finding of more shared features between two artifacts can contribute to an increase of confidence and certainty in the attribution of sameness. However, he points out that weaknesses in the use of analogy continue to exist. Determining the presence of shared features is still a subjective process that differs among researchers, and when seeking similarities between artifacts of different cultures, there may be no true relevance between them (pp. 150-152).

Lewis-Williams then proposes the use of what he refers to as "relations of relevance" rather than use of the traditional word "analogy." By this he means a "single relevant relation," such as a specific quality or behavior that could confidently be confirmed to be present in two differing cultures. Lewis-Williams uses the specific example of the human nervous system which has remained basically the same in all cultures from circa 40,000 BP until the present. Laboratory research has shown that certain geometric shapes appear in human awareness during altered states of consciousness. Lewis-Williams identifies these shapes in both contemporary African San Bushmen rock paintings and Paleolithic cave art. He then concludes that both of the artistic expressions were produced by tribal shamans during altered states of consciousness. However, Lewis-Williams admits that this modified version of analogical reasoning only provides the certainty that the images of both cultures originated in the conscious nervous system of the artists, and cannot guarantee that the two artifacts were made with the same intention or had the same meaning for the artists.

Some researchers generate theories by comparing historic cultural artifacts with prehistoric cultural artifacts across a gulf of time and space in an effort to find the cognitive intention and meaning for them. However, theories developed by the use of analogy usually furnish only a distraction and even erect a barrier to a more meaningful comprehension. Such researchers in most cases point out only a fanciful and superficial likeness, only an analogical comparison and not necessarily a true comprehension of the discussed phenomena.

Humans have been utilizing analogical reasoning for some length of time. The use of analogical thinking by Paleolithic Neanderthals and Homo sapiens enabled them to construct a relative though not accurate reality view. The earth for them was like a greater mother that brought forth life from within and where the dead human body was placed therein.

Caves also gave access to the womb of the earth from which life came. The caves were the place where gynocentric humans assisted the earth to give birth to the inchoate shapes that resembled animals by painting and petitioning the greater female mother to bring forth animal life to be hunted for food. The sculpted female figures and engraved and drawn vulva images are an anthropomorphic way of identifying what the earth was for them, a greater mother of life. While these were coherent analogical cognitive views for Paleolithic peoples, the analogies were not accurate or true and certainly in modern times are not apropos ways of thinking.

The use of analogy as a tool in an attempt to obtain reliable knowledge is, and will always be, fraught with risk and error. Therefore I have refrained from use of analogical reasoning in discussion, and when so doing, I call attention to this speculative and error prone way of thinking.

Chapter 3

Homo Neanderthalensis

The species Homo Neanderthalensis, or as a minority of researchers insist Homo sapiens neanderthalensis, produced the first expression of the longest-lasting religious view of humankind which endured circa 100,000-10,000 BP. Intentional Neanderthal burials that include offerings of flowers, tools, food remains, the mineral red ochre, and various curios, provide evidence to support this hypothesis. Having a brain similar to modern humans, tool-making skills, the capacity for speech, differing subsistence patterns that suggest planning, and the basic ability for making non-utilitarian objects and personal ornaments, Neanderthals possessed a basic and sufficient intelligence to develop a view regarding the origin of life and existence.

As a Homo species, Neanderthals possessed the perceptual capacities for animism, anthropomorphism, and dreaming, and the rudimentary ability to reason. Middle Paleolithic burial, begun by the Neanderthals and later practiced by modern Homo sapiens sapiens, is the first expression of what I consider to be a long-enduring earth cultus or religion. Burial is related to two other expressions of religion during the Upper Paleolithic which I will discuss in the chapters that follow, namely, cave art and the female figures.

My findings suggest that the intentional practice of Neanderthal burials began circa 100,000 BP and continued to the extinction of these early humans, circa 40,000-30,000 BP. To determine if the Neanderthals intentionally buried their dead, I will first focus on the earliest evidence for intentional human burial at Tabun and Qafzeh, and then the evidence of Shanidar cave. There is evidence in the Neanderthal remains of intentional burial at the archeological site of Shanidar cave, located in Iraq, as well as other locations in Europe and the Middle East. I have focused primarily on the Shanidar site, and briefly mention the secondary sites of La Chapelle in France, and Nahr Ibrahim Cave in Lebanon.

I have selected the Shanidar site for study based on two criteria. First, unlike many other excavations of Neanderthal remains in the past, investigators conducted a meticulous and detailed archeological investigation; and there are excellent records for this site. Secondly, there is a significant find associated with the site remains consisting of various identified flower varieties and particles of wood found beneath and around burial number IV.

The following characteristics serve briefly to introduce what is known of Homo Neanderthalensis. Neanderthals did not evolve in Africa but, rather, in Europe or western Asia (Tattersall, 1995, p. 73) and existed circa 200,000-30,000 BP. In Europe evidence suggests Neanderthals were the dominant species and were burying their dead according to specific rituals before the arrival of modern humans (Broglio, 1999) from the Middle East by circa 40,000 BP. The number of Neanderthals gradually declined to extinction. A Neanderthal lower jaw found in southern Spain has been dated by radiocarbon and uranium series tests to 30,000 BP, (Mellars, 1998, pp. 539-540) and a find of Neanderthal remains in the Vindija cave in Croatia has been radiocarbon dated to circa 29,000-28,000 BP (Neanderthal Museum, 2000).

The skeletal remains of over 1000 Neanderthals have been unearthed, more than any other species of early humans (Roos, 2000). According to investigation of Neanderthal living sites, as well as those of early modern human Upper Paleolithic sites, the average group size was approximately 25 persons (Hyland, 1993, pp. 707-710). Average height for male Neanderthals was 1.7 meters and weight on the average was 65 kilograms, whereas height for females was 1.6 meters and weight was an average of 50 kilograms (Stringer & Gamble, pp. 91-92). Considering the Neanderthal brain and the possible shape of vocal chords, some anthropologists assume Neanderthals had a rudimentary language (Stringer & Gamble, 1993, p. 90). Dental caries are absent from all known Neanderthal site remains (Trinkaus, 1983, p. 153). During the time of their existence in varying locations, the Neanderthals made and used 63 different kinds of flake tools and 21 variations of the handaxe (Tattersall, 1995, pp. 160-161).

Evidence of Earliest Intentional Burial

The earliest evidence of intentional burial by the human species occurs in the Middle East where Neanderthals and early modern humans are found in association. In what is modern-day Israel, some of the oldest burial remains of Neanderthals and of early Homo sapiens sapiens have been found at the cave sites of Tabun and Qafzeh. During the 1930's the skeletal remains of what has been identified as a 30 year old female Neanderthal, interred somewhat on the left side and in a loosely flexed body position (Garrod & Bate, 1937, p. 64) and an infant were excavated at the site of Tabun cave located in Israel (Bar-Yosef & Callander, 1999). The soil layer containing the remains has been dated using mass spectrometric U-series testing of bovid tooth enamel at the site, to circa 100,000 BP with a possible error of plus or minus 5,000 years (McDermott, Grun, Stringer, & Hawkesworth, 1993). Electron-spin resonance provided an approximate date of 110,000 BP for the remains (Shreeve, 1995). A uranium series method of dating using a sample of the mandible bone of the skeleton gave a possible range of dates for the remains from circa 34,000 BP plus or minus five thousand years to 70,000 BP plus or minus 25,000 years. The researchers of the study "recognized [the] uncertainties of U-series dating of bone," and that the range of dates is due to the uncertainty of the rate of uranium uptake by the fossils (Schwarcz, Simpson & Stringer, 1998). Using the thermoluminesence dating method, the flint tools in the layer containing the female skeletal remains of Tabun cave have been dated to circa 170,000 BP (Valladas, 1998, p. 72).

The partial remains of at least 20 hominids classified as Homo sapiens sapiens possessing archaic cranial features have been found at the site of Qafzeh cave located in the lower Galilee area of Israel. One of the skeletons was placed on its right side in a flexed position, and among the remains was found a pair of fallow deer antlers (Mellars, 1996, p. 380). The remains have been dated using isochron analysis to circa 90,000 BP (Valladas et al, 1998, p.71). Using thermoluminesence and electron-spin resonance dating gives varying dates between 90,000-100,000 BP.

The flexed body positions, the presence of an infant and antlers suggest intentional burial at both sites. However, circa 100,000 BP there exists no convincing evidence of burial offerings such as tools, animal bones, and ochre. Speth & Tchernov (1998) observe that in the remains of the early Homo sapiens sapiens found to date in the Mideast, the artifact evidence has failed to produce "clear evidence of grave offerings or art," and their stone tools resemble those of the Neanderthals (p. 224). Not until after 40,000 BP when artifact evidence supports the view that Homo sapiens sapiens had ventured into the continent of Europe (Brown, 2001) is there convincing evidence of burial offerings (Harrold, 1980) and therefore more convincingly the presence of a religious view of existence. This surprising finding at least suggests the possibility that the intellectually superior Homo sapiens sapiens, in this one unique behavior of burial, learned from and were influenced by the culture of Homo Neanderthalensis. However, for researchers, the most probable and acceptable view is that the practice of burial and the placing of offerings therein was independently developed by Homo sapiens sapiens.

The earliest undisputable skeletal evidence of modern humans in Europe consists of skull remains found in Germany that have been carbon-dated to circa 31,000 BP. However, no artifacts of intentional burial or grave offerings were associated with this find (Brown, 2001). The evidence of the earliest intentional burials by Homo sapiens sapiens associated with grave offerings of red ochre and pierced shells date from circa 28,000 in Portugal (Holden, 1999) and range from circa 27,000-22,000 BP in Sungir, Russia; Dolni Vestonice, Moravia; and the Gower Peninsula, Wales (Pettitt, 1999).

However, at Shanidar cave in Iraq, evidence does exist for intentional burial and grave offerings, dated to circa 60,000 BP (Solecki, 1975) and therefore the evidence at least suggests that a religious view existed by this time and possibly extended back to the earliest intentional human burials circa 100,000 BP.

Evidence of Shanidar Cave

Prior to discussion of the archaeological contents found in Shanidar cave located in Northeast Iraq, I will briefly mention some impressive features that may been of interest to early Neanderthals. On the lower side base of a rock cliff face of a mountain, the cave opening is roughly by my estimate 27 meters (90 feet) wide, 8 meters (25 feet) high, inside almost 14 meters (45 feet) at its highest point, and 40 meters (130 feet) from front to the back of the cave. Two large holes in the cave ceiling open to the sky above. They uncannily resemble a pair of human eyes looking into the cave from above. While the impressive ocular-like openings exist today, they may or may not have existed in the cave during Neanderthal occupation.

Beginning in 1951, the remains of nine Neanderthals were found at Shanidar. Since only a small portion of the cave floor has been excavated, it is probable there are more Neanderthal remains to be recovered at the site (Trinkaus & Shipman, 1993, p. 338). The first discovery was of an infant whose remains measured 3.8 decimeters in length, and whose legs and arms were in a flexed position with the skull facing upwards (Solecki, 1971, pp. 100-102).

Four of the Neanderthal site remains in the cave were attributed to unintentional burial by rock falls. Ceiling portions of the cave dislodged, perhaps due to earthquakes, and crushed the unfortunate individuals (p. 191). However, the sites located in 1960, "Shanidar IV [male] and VI [female] and associated remains and the Shanidar baby were found under conditions which indicate and suggest purposeful burial" (p. 191). By associated remains, Solecki meant the few partial remains of sites VII, a female, and VIII, the second infant.

Among the items found in the site of the first discovered infant remains in 1953 was a small block of limestone near the left heel. Near this was a piece of carbon substance that measured 12.8 by 19.2 millimeters. While not commenting on the quality, Solecki mentions that a large flint was found 5.1 centimeters from the east side of the skull. A small piece of mammal bone was found near the left knee, and a fragment of burnt bone lay near the right arm. A fire bed was located 41 centimeters above the infant's remains.

Solecki remarks that these objects and features apparently were associated with the normal occupational layer and not intentionally placed with the infant's remains. However, he then adds that it is at least possible that the articles were burial offerings (1971, p. 102). Using a combination of carbon-dating and stratigraphy (p. 181) this find dates to circa 70,000 BP (Solecki, 1957).

After the find of the Shanidar infant, Solecki and T. Dale Stewart, during the 1956-57 season, discovered Shanidar I remains, dated to circa 45,000 BP, of a 40 year-old-male killed by a rock fall.
Solecki conjectures that companions of the man saw what had occurred and soon afterward heaped portable-size stones over the body. This heap of stones was clearly distinguished and differed from areas of normal rock falls found during the course of the excavation (p. 139). Small mammal bones were found on the top and among this pile of stones. It is possible that the bones were placed there during a funeral ritual for the deceased (p. 141).

At the Shanidar III site of skeletal remains, there was also a male unmistakably killed by a rock fall from the cave ceiling. No human intervention or presence that could have occurred after the death of this adult male Neanderthal was observed during the excavation. The remains of the Shanidar II site dating to circa 60,000 BP indicate a male Neanderthal was also killed by a rock fall. There is evidence that, after this event, companions of the man placed a small collection of stones over the body and lit a large fire above it (p. 164). In this fire hearth there were Neanderthal stone points. Solecki comments that one of the points was lying directly in contact with and over another point. He emphatically states that it was hardly accidental. A number of broken and split mammal bones found at the site were, according to Solecki, possible remains of a funeral offering (pp. 162-163).

Shanidar V dating to circa 45,000 BP, was found near Shanidar I and III. Death of the individual who might have been a male appeared to be caused by a rock fall as evidenced by broken and crushed bones. Some of the bones were displaced, indicating disturbance of the site by later residents of the cave. Not long after death, a fire was built over the deceased remains.

A large lower jaw of a mammal, possibly a deer, was found close to the skull remains and hearth perhaps indicating a burial offering (p. 171).

Shanidar IV, VI, VII, and VIII were discovered in 1960 in close proximity to each other. The remains of Shanidar IV were those of a male in a fully flexed position with legs and arms folded close to the body lying on its left side. Among and near the remains were mammal bones. Solecki, as with all the other sites, took six soil samples from within and around the skeletal remains.

Three of the samples yielded unusual amounts of flower pollen. To the side of this site were found the remains of Shanidar VI, reported to be an adult female. Intermingled with these remains was also the partial skeleton of another adult female Shanidar VII; and below these, interred first, were the remains of another infant, subsequently labeled Shanidar VIII. Solecki comments that the bones of burial VI and VII were not in articulation and were only partially present, suggesting that the remains were a secondary interment (pp. 167, 169).

In 1968, a selection of soil samples from the remains of site IV found in the Shanidar cave was tested by palynologist, Arlette Leroi-Gourhan (1975). The samples and skeletal remains had been found enclosed by a boundary of stones. Of the 28 different pollen grains identified, seven of them were in clusters, including the anthers of the flower and led her to conclude that whole flowers were introduced inside the cave at the same time. One of the pollen samples even included the wing scale of a butterfly. Neither birds, tunneling rodents, nor the remains of coprolites can explain the presence of the flowers located inside the cave at least 15 meters from the entrance (pp. 562- 563).

Leroi-Gourhan mentions that it was confirmed by Solecki during excavation that the soil of the grave appeared to be different from the soil above and around the skeleton. Not only was the soil richer in pollen, but small pieces of wood were also detected (p. 563).

These were identified as Ephedra, a small woody plant whose branches as evidenced by the remains were woven into a bedding on which the deceased was laid. Other identified flowers include Achillea (yarrow), Centaurea cyanus (cornflower), Centaurea solstitialis (St. Barnaby's thistle), Senecio varieties (ragwort or groundsel), Muscari (grape hyacinth), and Althaea (hollyhock). These varieties of flowering plants continue to grow in Iraq today (Solecki, 1975, pp. 880-881). Leroi-Gourhan (1975) implies that the flowering plants were chosen for aesthetic value, the brilliant blue and yellow were placed upon the deceased.

The selection of plants placed in the Shanidar IV site was probably a result of the time of year. These plants bloom today during the months of May and June; and assuming a near or similar climate, the male Neanderthal was interred during these months over 50,000 years ago (p. 564).

Originally Solecki (1972) also thought that the presence of flowers at the Shanidar site indicated an aesthetic intention. However, after the flowering plants were shown to have medicinal potential, he favored the view that this known potential for healing was probably why they had been placed with the remains (Solecki, 1975). The flowers found at the Shanidar IV site have also been examined for medical and/or pharmacological properties. The Achillea or Yarrow species of flower still found in the Zagros Mountains of Iraq today contain oils that have been shown to have anti-inflammatory effects. The plant Centaurea solstitialis has been shown to have antiseptic properties that inhibit bacterial growth. The Senecio species have a number of alkaloids that exhibit hemostyptic, astringent, and deliriant effects.

Muscari evidences some properties of hepatotoxic, diuretic, and possible deliriant activity. Ephedra compounds display anti-inflammatory activity and the plant also contains the alkaloid ephedrine, which has been shown to have stimulating amphetamine, therapeutic, and euphoric effects on the central nervous system. Althea officinalis shows antimicrobial and anti-inflammatory effects (Lietava, 1992, p. 264).

Lietava suggests that, rather than aesthetics or the season, the recently discovered therapeutic or curative effects of the various flowering plants was the main determinant for their presence in the Shanidar IV burial site. Pharmacological content known by the Neanderthals might have resulted in the intention to use these particular plants as a curative way of endowing the deceased with life (p. 265).

The most convincing evidence for purposeful burial at Shanidar is the find at site IV dated to circa 60,000 BP. The soil above and around the remains was of a different composition, suggesting disturbance as a result of excavation. The unusually large quantities of flower pollen and traces of wood in relation to the remains strongly suggest intentional placement by humans. The selection of flowers for the interment was originally thought to be solely a concern for the aesthetics of color or the growing season, but follow-up research has shown that all of the plants exhibit medicinal or curative properties. An accumulation of so many therapeutic plants occurring randomly in a single isolated location would be statistically improbable.

After considering the evidence and comments by researchers, I would argue that intentional burial at Shanidar by Neanderthals is evident. The unintentional burials due to rock falls were clearly distinguished from the intentional burials of sites IV, VI, VII, VIII, and the other infant, which appear to suggest purposeful burial. The findings of multiple infant, male and female adult articulated remains spanning thousands of years in flexed body positions, accompanied by flower pollen, flint tools, fire-hearths, burnt and non-burnt animal bones that suggest funeral offerings, all support the view that interment was intentional at Shanidar.

While there is convincing evidence that Neanderthals did intentionally bury their dead, Gargett (1989) argues that based on the written excavation records of six Neanderthal burial sites, including Shanidar, there is an absence of clear stratigraphic evidence for intentional burial. At Shanidar IV, the soil stratum immediately surrounding the remains showed no clear evidence of difference from the naturally occurring vertical and horizontal deposits of sediment.

Gargett argues that the investigators had a prior subjective view that intentional burial was a strong possibility (p. 176). Regarding the find of flower pollen in the Shanidar IV grave, Gargett's view is that, since the cave entrance of Shanidar is so large, a forceful wind probably carried the flowers into the cave along with twigs and branches. He also mentions that rodents are another strong probability for transporting flower pollen into the area of the skeletal remains; burrowing tunnels of gerbils were found throughout the Shanidar excavation site.

For Gargett, the finding of at least some nearly complete Neanderthal skeletons in the Middle Paleolithic is evidence that something was happening to preserve the few complete specimens in the fossil remains. However, rather than attribute this anomaly to intentional burial, he suggests the remains are a result of natural burial due to geological processes over time such, as weathering, cave or rock-shelter collapse, water erosion, and sediment deposit (p. 157). Since Neanderthals lived in caves and rock shelters in which most skeletons have been found, the sheltering confines would have contributed to the preservation of Neanderthal remains. Gargett insists that the so-called intentional burials are actually natural burials, a result of having died in a protected cave area, as a result of a catastrophic cave collapse, or the body eventually coming to rest in a natural depression of the cave that became a sediment trap.

Smirnov argues that Gargett ignores the "non-natural character of the burials" and "proposes sophisticated geological scenarios featuring almost every logically possible agent except human beings" (Kooijmans, Smirnov, Solecki, Villa, Weber, & Gargett, 1989, p. 323).

Smirnov also poses other questions. How can Gargett explain a lack of nearly complete or articulated skeletons during the Lower Paleolithic and the fairly large number of articulated skeletons of adults and children dating to the Middle Paleolithic? Why did the natural processes arrange the bodies on their right side and oriented transverse to the entrance of the shelter, regardless of the site orientation (Kooijmans et al, p. 323)?

Gargett argues that there was a lack of vertical and horizontal stratigraphic evidence of a disturbed stratum that would suggest intentional excavation of Shanidar IV remains. Solecki responds, "The sediment around the skeleton seemed to be lighter in weight and looser above and around the Shanidar IV skeleton than the sediment below, which was loamy and tough. This would indicate disturbance" (Kooijmans et al, p. 324).

Gargett's remark that the Shanidar IV site shows a lack of good stratigraphic evidence for intentional burial is not accurate, as Solecki did identify a difference, at least in terms of compactness, between the soil layers of the cave and the soil containing the skeletal remains (Leroi-Gourhan, 1975, p. 563; Kooijmans et al, 1989, p. 324). The view that the wind carried the flowers and branches to the site of the skeletal remains is unlikely, since the wind did not blow them into any other site.

Soil samples were taken from other site remains, but no unusual amount of pollen or wood was discovered. As for rodent transport of these plant remains, Solecki remarks on where gerbils were found at the other sites. However, he does not mention any evidence of rodent presence, burrowing tunnels, or disturbance in or immediately surrounding the remains of Shanidar IV. Gargett's view that all of the skeletal remains at Shanidar were natural burials due to cave collapse or death in a protected area that gradually filled up as a result of sedimentation processes is not convincing. At Shanidar, Solecki clearly distinguishes between unintentionally and intentionally interred remains. Also, even in protected areas of the caves, predators such as hyenas would have likely found and consumed the remains before the sedimentation processes occurred.

Other Neanderthal site remains that contain evidence of intentional burial and offerings include La Chapelle in France (Riel-Salvatore & Clark, 2001) and Nahr Ibrahim Cave in Lebanon.

Grave offerings were intentionally placed at the La Chapelle site where the articulated skeleton of a 50-year-old male Neanderthal dated to circa 45,000 BP (Man of Neanderthal Museum, 2000) was discovered with the right arm flexed in an upright position and alongside of this arm was the complete leg of a bison, a number of tools shaped from flint, and several red ochre lumps (Maringer, 1960, pp. 23-24). Animal bones were also found placed on the skull and surrounded by pieces of jasper and quartz (Wreshner, 1976, p.718).

During the 1970's Solecki (1975) and others excavated the Nahr Ibrahim Cave in Lebanon, a Neanderthal habitation site dated to circa 52,000 BP. They found over 325,000 flint tools, cores, and flakes and what Solecki describes as the ritual burial of a fallow deer. Remains included long leg bones, foot bones, a large section of articulated vertebrate, and the skull placed on top of these. Sprinkled in the remains were also small pieces of red ochre. Solecki comments that the ochre was definitely out of place in this particular environment, and was most likely obtained from a heavy ochre deposit located at a distance to the northeast of the cave burial site (p. 290).

According to Chase & Dibble (1987) only 33 percent of Middle Paleolithic burials contain some kind of grave offerings, whereas 88 percent of Upper Paleolithic burials have them. Chase & Dibble and other researchers agree that intentional burial by modern humans was certainly a practice. Their argument is based on the same criteria of what is found, though sparsely, in Neanderthal site remains. These include grave offerings, stone tools, burnt and non-burnt animal bones, and red ochre. Mellars (1996) accepts that there was an intentional burial by anatomically modern humans at Qafzeh, Israel, based on what he characterizes as "symbolic grave offerings" that consist only of a pair of fallow deer antlers found with the remains (p. 380).

In conclusion, at least some of the humans known as Homo Neanderthalensis did intentionally bury their dead.

The flowers in the Shanidar IV site remains, and the flint tools, red ochre, and curios of jasper and quartz found in the La Chapelle and Nahr Ibrahim remains, also confirm that offerings were placed on, beneath, and around the body of intentional Neanderthal burials.

Intention and Intelligence

I have presented evidence that the Neanderthals did bury their dead. The question I pose now is, what was the intention for this behavior, and were they intelligent enough to develop a religious view? Generally, researchers advocate hygiene or emotional bonds as probable intentions for burial, and insist that Neanderthal intelligence did not allow for much more than this.

Tattersall (1995) argues that no other archaic humans before Neanderthals buried their dead; Neanderthals did bury their dead, at least occasionally, and the intention for this behavior was most likely to dispose of bodies that would have cluttered the living area and attracted predators (pp. 169-170). Stringer & Gamble (1993) also think that the intention for Neanderthal burial was probably more related to corpse disposal (p. 160).

While hygiene concerns seem a possible intention for Neanderthal burial, as it at least explains the presence of articulated remains and flexed legs and arms, it does not satisfactorily account for the grave offerings of stone tools, the animal bones of possible food offerings, fire hearths close to the skeletal remains, and the presence of flower pollen in burial IV at Shanidar.

Stringer & Gamble (1993) report that the Shanidar I site remains of a male had head injury and trauma to the right side of the body, perhaps from a crushing rock fall. This individual probably experienced infection and partial paralysis and blindness in the left eye. Examination of the remains determined that the individual was disabled, but he lived on for several years, aided by his fellow Neanderthals.

Shanidar III site remains showed evidence of a healed rib wound, while Shanidar V showed evidence of a serious scalp injury that had healed while living. (p. 4) Shackley (1980) observes that the care provided for the injured and old suggests a concern for the individual (p. 112). Dibble & Chase (1993) think the intention for Neanderthal burial was an emotional bond among group members (p. 172). Geist (1978) also thinks that the intention for Neanderthal burials was a result of emotional bonds. Through the cooperation necessary for group survival, close emotional bonds would have formed among the members, contributing to affectionate care of the body after death (p. 320).

While reasonable, the view that emotional bonds provided the only intention for burial does not seem satisfactory when considering Homo erectus, the hominid species that preceded the Neanderthals. Homo erectus as one of the most successful hominid species, evolved in Africa 1.8 million years ago and eventually migrated to Europe and Asia and even to the island of Java, where this species survived until 30,000 BP (Gibbons, 1998, p. 1637). They lived in groups, used fire, (Eliade, 1978, p. 4) and probably had a rudimentary language (Ruspoli, 1986, p. 12). Homo erectus made and used stone tools and wood throwing spears, and constructed dwellings or hut structures (Gore, 1997, pp. 101-111; Angela & Angela, 1993, p. 180; Tattersall, 1995, p. 72).

With Homo erectus' ability to use fire, make stone tools and spears, live collectively, and build shelters, this evolved intelligence of thousands of years would have surely developed social and emotional bonds. In nearly two million years of evolution and group living, there must have been emotional bonds present. Even domestic and wild animals observed today form emotional bonds. Yet there are no known intentional Homo erectus burials. No known intentional burials have been found from the Lower Paleolithic (Harrold, 1980, p. 195) which dates from circa 3 to 2 million to 150,000 BP. Not until the Middle Paleolithic, circa 150,000-40,000 BP, does there appear evidence of intentional burials.

It seems certain that Homo erectus had emotions as well as some social and technological intelligence as evidenced in collective living and hunting and the crafting of tools, spears, and shelters. In my view, there were no Homo erectus burials because they had no conceived idea that the origin of life came from the interior of the earth as did the Neanderthals.

Dibble and Chase (1993) accept the evidence for intentional burials by Neanderthals at no less than nine sites, including the Shanidar site (p. 170). Yet they think the intention for these burials was due to personal affection, perhaps respect for the dead, and protection of the deceased from scavengers and weather. In their view, Neanderthals did not have the intelligence to attribute a symbolic and therefore a religious meaning to the act of burial (p. 172).

However, my argument is that the Neanderthals did have the necessary intelligence and were capable of rudimentary reasoning or symbolic thinking, and further they did have a concern for the origin or beginning of existence or a religious view. The definition of symbol is "something that stands for or suggests something else." For Stringer & Gamble (1993) symbolism involves mental substitutions and associations between people, objects, and contexts. Since Neanderthals had differing subsistence behavioral patterns of both scavenging and hunting, both of these behaviors show evidence of planning, since they had to make choices of where to move and when (p. 203).

The brain size of the Neanderthals was at least equal to and similar to modern humans (Hyland, 1993, p. 709-710). It would seem that the Neanderthals must have had at least some basic ability for symbolic ideas or concepts. Chase & Dibble (1987) think so, and conclude that it is highly probable that Neanderthals did have some weakly developed capacity for symbolism (p. 285).

Some researchers think the Neanderthals had the ability to speak. Considering the Neanderthal brain and the possible shape of vocal chords, Neanderthals probably had a rudimentary language (Stringer & Gamble, 1993, p. 90).

In a cave discovered in 1990 at Bruniquel in south France, carbon-dated to circa 47,600 BP, investigators found a burned piece of bear bone used as fuel in the context remains of a structure built by Neanderthals. The structure measures four by five meters and is constructed of pieces of stalactite and stalagmite, located approximately 400 meters from the entrance of the cave. Construction so far underground shows a sophisticated use of fire and also suggests some sort of language ability by those who constructed it, as communication was probably used to coordinate the efforts of the workers (Balter, 1996, p. 449).

At recent excavations at Gorhan Cave located in Gibraltar, researchers have discovered a geometric "cross-hatching" carved into the bedrock of the cave by Neanderthals dating to a minimum of 39,000 BP. A pointed stone tool was used to repeatedly and intentionally engrave the design to be viewed by others. The researchers state, "The production of purposely made painted or engraved designs on cave walls is recognized as a major cognitive step in human evolution, considered exclusive to modern humans." Further the researchers conclude, "This discovery demonstrates the capacity of the Neanderthals for abstract thought and expression through the use of geometric forms." (Vidal-Rodriguez, J., d'Errico, F. Pacheco, F. A., Blasco, R. Rosell, J., Jennings, R. P., Queffelec, A., Finlayson, G., Fa, D. A., Lopez, J. M. G., Carrion, J. S., Negro, J. J., Finlayson, S. Caceres, L. M., Bernal, M. A., Jimenez, S. F, 2014).

Evidence of the rudimentary ability to make and use symbols has also been discovered at the Neanderthal site of Bacho Kiro, Bulgaria. Carbon-dated to circa 44,000 BP a non-utilitarian bone fragment engraved with a zigzag design was found that was clearly not the result of work or cutting marks, but rather the creation of an intentional design. This same zigzag motif is found frequently among the later Upper Paleolithic era artifacts of non-utilitarian bone fragments, tools, and usually associated with engraved and painted animals of cave art. The designs are unquestionably similar, and this particular piece of Neanderthal worked bone was coated with ochre after engraving, further suggesting its symbolic significance (Marshack, 1976, p. 277).

A shaped mammoth tooth artifact just over 10 centimeters in length was recovered from a Neanderthal site at Tata, Hungary, dated to circa 50,000 BP. The section of the molar was cut, carved, and beveled to make it almost a complete oval shape. Microscopic examination revealed that the work was worn smooth as if from long handling, and that, at least once and perhaps many times, it had been painted with red ochre. For Marshack this is convincing evidence of the making of a symbolic artifact plainly intended for long-term usage, and evidence that the artisan had planned for a non-utilitarian symbolic use of the object (pp. 277-278).

Chase & Dibble (1987) call attention to the relatively few finds of Neanderthal art. Neanderthal artifacts, such as bi-face tools; a mammoth tooth carefully shaped into an oval; perforated, punctured, and grooved animal teeth and bone; and some remains of red ochre usage, are considered to be the expressions of an aesthetic sense for regularity and symmetry. Chase & Dibble think the Neanderthals did not have sufficient intelligence to intend a symbolic and ritual use for the non-utilitarian artifacts.

However, I agree with Mithen (1994) who points out that Neanderthal intelligence was probably characterized by three general cognitive domains of mental ability that include "social, technical, and natural history intelligence." Social intelligence developed during the course of group living and consisted of complex social interactions (p. 33). The similarity of artifacts such as handaxes among different Neanderthal groups is evidence of cooperation and the shared ability for imitation. The skilled stone-working of the Neanderthal Levallois style displays a level of technical intelligence that is not inferior to that of modern humans (Mithen, 1994, p. 33).

Mithen defines natural history intelligence as the "cognitive abilities used in the interaction with animals and plants." Since Neanderthals ranged as far as Russia and Siberia, it can be inferred a sophisticated level of natural history intelligence that would have been necessary to live in colder climates.

Another characteristic of natural history intelligence is the anticipating and predicting of the movement of animals. While admitting this ability is debatable among the Neanderthals, the faunal remains of southwestern France suggest a substantial amount of large game hunting in contrast to scavenging (Mithen, 1994, p. 34). Overall, Mithen concludes there is evidence the Neanderthals possessed the ability to imitate, to arrange an order of things, and to form rudimentary categories.

Commenting on the finds of intentional Neanderthal burials, animal bones arranged therein, flowers present as in the case of the Shanidar IV skeleton, and pieces of red ochre sometimes found in living sites, Marshack (1976) remarks, “The sense one gets from these data and interpretations is of a struggling, seminal, almost mute awareness of death and a kind of incipient proto-symbolism” (p. 276).

My view is that based upon a similarity of brain size with Homo sapiens sapiens, the use of speech, the engraving of a geometric form on a cave surface, the making of non-utilitarian objects (such as the shaped mammoth tooth coated with ochre, zigzag design, and personal ornaments), the skilled technical ability for the Levallois method of stone-working shared by proto-Homo sapiens sapiens until circa 40,000 BP, and the ability to anticipate and predict the movement of game animals thereby planning where and when to move; there is convincing evidence of Neanderthal intelligence and the ability for abstract thought, rudimentary reasoning, and use of symbols. Therefore they also had the ability to develop a rudimentary religious view.

Commenting on two of the common features of Neanderthal remains, Shackley (1980) observes that hearth fires are often found in close proximity with Neanderthal remains. She does not see the presence of fires as a random placement, but assumes that the fires were intentionally lit after burial. She speculates that the fire might represent a ritual element such as providing warmth to counteract the chill of death, and is more likely to be the remains of a funeral feast fire lit while last rites were being carried out (pp. 103-104).

Shackley thinks that the burnt animal bones often found in proximity to Neanderthal skeletal remains represent a last offering of food for the departed. Shackley suggests that Neanderthals had a religious view and performed religious rituals. After investigating Neanderthal remains, I agree with Shackley that the evidence suggests that the intention for Neanderthal burials was religious.

Discussion

Having examined the physical evidence of Neanderthal remains, the offerings associated with them, the views of other researchers as to the intention for these interments, and determining that the Neanderthals did have the necessary intelligence for rudimentary reasoning, I have concluded that the essential meaning for the behavior of Neanderthal burial consists of three main points:

1. The act of burial was a meaningful interaction with the earth.
2. The intention for Neanderthal burial was to place the body where life originated, the interior of the earth.
3. Neanderthal burial is therefore the earliest evidence of religion.

To support this insight into the essential meaning of Neanderthal burial, I began to investigate the cognitive processes that could have contributed to the phenomenon. As I have defined it, religion consists of the human intention to find one's way back to the beginning and to reconnect to the origin of life. The artifact evidence suggests that the Neanderthals viewed the interior of the earth as the origin of life, based upon their observation of the environment; the perceptual processes of animism, anthropomorphism, and dreams; and rudimentary conceptual reasoning.

Foraging for plants and roots as food, Neanderthals would have observed that these living forms had an origin from and grew out of the interior of the earth. They might have also observed and known that vegetation came from seed. Neanderthals would have surely observed plants appearing from the soil and growing day by day, and insects and animals coming from holes and dens in the earth.

The force of growth present in living things coming from the earth would have resulted in the animistic perception that the earth was alive.

The cave provided an access to the mysterious interior of the earth. Profoundly dark, eerily quiet and with unusual interior noises of wind and dripping or running water, damp, a constant temperature between 50-55 degrees Fahrenheit the cave appeared in sharp contrast to the environment of the ground above. The large opening of the cave was an unusual feature, an exception to the natural surface of soil and stone. The cave opening and interior exceeded the natural and was preternatural, even supernatural.

During burial the body was placed in the earth where the life of plants, insects, burrowing animals, and hibernating animals such as the bears originated. Seeing plants grow from the earth, the young of insects and animals born from and alive within the earth, the Neanderthals placed the deceased in the ground, suggesting an expression of an animistic perception and desire that, just as the young plants and animals came forth repeatedly from the earth, so the deceased could in some way be restored to life.

Anthropomorphism is defined as the attribution of human qualities to nonhuman things or events. This innate subconscious perceptual process occurs as a spontaneous and subconscious interpretive tendency to find significance or meaning (Gutherie, 1993, pp. 3, 7). For Mithen (1994) what marked the transition from the Middle to the Upper Paleolithic era circa 35,000 BP was the evolved human cognitive ability for anthropomorphism, attributing mental processes such as intentions or thoughts to nature and to animals. Mithen (1996) argues that the Neanderthals had an "intuitive belief-desire psychology...as well developed as it is in the modern mind....Yet we have no evidence that this was projected onto non-intentional objects, as it is for modern humans," (p. 717) through anthropomorphic thinking.

However, I would argue that the Neanderthals did perceive anthropomorphically, at least on a rudimentary level. This is evident in their use of the mineral red ochre.

Red ochre is the common name for iron hematite, a naturally occurring mineral ranging in colors of red to brown. That early humans were attracted to and used red ochre more than any other mineral is significant. Evidence exists for the use of ochre by Homo erectus at four sites prior to 100,000 BP (Wreshner, 1985, p. 388). However, there is scant evidence to show symbolic usage. The presence of ochre at these sites could be due to natural occurrences or could have been brought to the site as a curio (Marshack, 1981).

Recently at the early Homo sapies sapiens site known as Blombos Cave in South Africa, over 8,000 pieces of ochre were discovered, many showing evidence of being utilized in some fashion. Nine of the small shaped red ochre pieces that date to circa 77,000 BP show evidence of being engraved with cross-hatched geometric designs (Henshilwood et al, 2002). There is evidence of ochre usage in southwestern Australia circa 60,000 BP (Stringer, 2000).

There is also evidence of the use of red ochre by Neanderthals at 17 sites circa 50,000-30,000 BP. From 50,000-30,000 BP evidence does exist for the symbolic use of red ochre by Neanderthals in both human and animal burials and was most likely associated with blood (Wreschner, 1985, p. 388-389). This evidence occurs at the Neanderthal sites of La Chapelle-aux-Saints and Nahr Ibrahim. In La Chapelle, ochre might have been a personal belonging of the deceased or been offered as a funeral gift to be used in the netherworld; just as the Nahr Ibrahim ochre in the ritual inhumation of the Fallow Deer might have been conceived as symbolizing the procreation of these beasts, on whose meat the population of hunters depended (p. 393).

Wreshner (1976) thinks that the use of red ochre sprinkled on the body or bedding of Neanderthal remains suggests a symbolic association of the color red with the necessary blood of life (p.718). I agree with Wreshner that the veins or deposits of red ochre found in the earth were most likely associated with the blood of life.

Support for this view can be found in the Neanderthal behavior of intentionally placing red ochre in the interred remains of an animal and humans. Placing red ochre with the interred remains at least suggests a rudimentary anthropomorphic perception. The mineral red ochre was the only naturally occurring substance having the color that resembled blood. Observing that blood flowed from the body of the female Neanderthal during her monthly menstruation, and that during the event of birth there was the presence of much blood, Neanderthal's associated red ochre primarily with the blood of menstruation and the birth of life. Neanderthals also surely had the intelligence to recognize that when blood flowed from the body during an injury to a human or animal, that the blood was no longer in the body and not having blood brought death. Adding the red ochre to burial sites was most likely an expression of the desire to restore life or health to the deceased. The use of red ochre was an expression of anthropomorphically perceiving it to resemble human blood.

Like animism and anthropomorphism, dreams are an innate subconscious perceptual process that prehistoric peoples would have had in common with modern humans. Dreams occur without any conscious intention; nor can dreams be prevented. The mental images of dreams occur in the cerebral cortex and are often the result of emotional concerns (Hartmann, 1999, pp. 64-66). Since Neanderthals and Upper Paleolithic humans had both cerebral cortex and emotions, they must have experienced dreams.

Tylor (1958) thought that early historic humans were puzzled by two biological problems: What makes the difference between a dead body and a living one, and what are the human shapes appearing in dreams (p. 12)? He states that early humans thought that these images were the phantoms, ghosts, animating spirits, or souls of deceased relatives, friends, even animals, and that this disembodied entity was seen in dreams. Tylor thought this experience was interpreted by early humans as a spiritual realm differing from material existence, paving the way for early religion.

However, as the behavioral evidence of burial suggests, it is more useful to rephrase Tylor's question as to what prehistoric humans might have asked themselves to, "where" are these human shapes that appear in dreams? The relationship of dreams with darkness could have contributed to the intention for human burials under the soil surface of the earth and in caves. If dreams came during the night, where was it always night? Through observation, it was known that it was always dark under the earth from where the plants grew and in the crevices and dens where insects and animals lived and had young, and it was especially dark when entering into the preternatural opening of caves.

Early humans very likely thought the images of deceased humans came from or were located in the dark interior of the earth accessible through the cave. The interring of the human body within the earth after the ending of human life could have been perceived as a way of returning it to the origin of life, and where the image of the deceased was located when it appeared during nightly dreams.

Reasoning by analogy consists of an association, relating this with that. Imitation in tool making by Homo erectus, Neanderthals, and Homo sapiens sapiens suggests that early humans possessed an ability to recognize similarity. Neanderthals used 63 types of flake tools (Chase & Dibble, 1987, p. 271) and this ability would have necessitated a learned set of purposeful behaviors, planning, and a talent for imitation, of making one tool like another. This suggests a developing ability for rudimentary analogical reasoning as well. Rudimentary reasoning would then have made use of animistic, anthropomorphic, and dream perceptions to further form conscious concepts that the earth was alive, was the origin of life, and was where the dead resided when they appeared in dreams during the darkness of the night. When the Neanderthals experienced helplessness in preventing the ending of human life, their conceived strategy of burial was to return the lifeless form to where life was observed to originate. In this way, humans found their way back to and reconnected to the origin of existence; the earth. Thus began the first and longest enduring religion of humankind.

Prior to Neanderthals, there is no archeological evidence of Homo erectus burials or the presence of grave offerings of any kind. While no evidence of anything resembling a Homo erectus burial has been found to date, there is the interesting site of La Sima de los Huesos in Spain, where in 1993, the remains of approximately 32 Homo erectus individuals were found in a cave dating to circa 300,000 BP. The remains were mainly young adults or teenagers, who seem to have been thrown down a shaft into the cave during some sort of ritual. Three skulls were found, one of which had a brain size equal to a modern human (Gore, 1997, pp. 111-112). Based on skull and skeletal size Barham (1999) labels the remains at this site as "proto-Neanderthals." While there seems to be no suggestion of intentional burial at this site, intention certainly seems to be present in some form as an explanation for the accumulation of so many skeletal remains.

In Homo erectus remains there is no evidence of burials or grave offerings, while 33 percent of Neanderthal remains contain grave offerings, and 88 percent of modern human remains from circa 30,000-10,000 BP contain grave offerings (Chase &Dibble, 1987, p. 273). This data indicates a progressive development from no apparent interest in the human corpse to a modest concern and finally to a fully developed burial practice. The essential meaning of this progression is that Homo erectus did not have a religious view of the earth as origin; this view was first developed by Homo Neanderthalensis, and then later practiced by Homo sapiens sapiens.

I would agree with Renfrew (1994) that religion involves a shared system of views that seeks to provide answers to existential questions. These questions include: Where do we come from? Where are we going? Religion also consists of the following characteristics (pp. 48, 51):

1. It implies an experience of the supernatural or that which is above or transcends nature or the natural.
2. Transcendence does not actually imply separation, and does not have to be abstract and separate, but may be numinously concrete and physically present.

3. When religious ritual occurs, it is usually located at the boundary between this world and another, a supernatural world.
4. One of the archaeological indicators of ritual is that it is usually performed at a site having natural beauty or appeal, such as in a cave.
5. Other relevant indicators of ritual are the offerings of food, drink, or other objects.

All of these features are present at Neanderthal site remains. The Neanderthal burials suggest that for the first time humans recognized the origin of life to be the earth.

Conclusion

After having examined the physical evidence of Neanderthal remains, the offerings associated with them, the views of other researchers as to the intention for these interments, and determining that the Neanderthals did have the necessary intelligence for rudimentary reasoning, I reached the following conclusions.

The human species Homo Neanderthalensis began the first expression of the longest-lasting religious view that subsequently endured circa 100,000-10,000 BP. Evidence to support this hypothesis can be found in intentional Neanderthal burials that include offerings of flowers, tools, food remains, red ochre, and various curios. Having a brain size similar to modern humans, and based upon their tool-making skills, capacity for speech, differing subsistence patterns that suggest planning, and the basic ability for making non-utilitarian objects and personal ornaments, Neanderthals possessed enough basic intelligence to develop views about the origin of life and existence.

The artifact evidence suggests that Neanderthals undoubtedly possessed the innate perceptual capacities for animism, anthropomorphism, and dreaming, as well as a rudimentary ability for analogical reasoning.

Observing the phenomenon of various plants growing from the earth, insects and animals coming from and living in dens within the earth, the awe-inspiring physical presence of caves leading into the depths of the earth, the Neanderthals would have perceived and conceived the interior of the earth to be the origin of life and existence. When Neanderthals experienced the poignancy of the death of a child or adult, little could be done. The deceased could not be put back into the body of the mother from which the human life had come. The only recourse was to place the deceased where it was observed that most of life came from, the interior of the earth.

The act of burial was a meaningful interaction with the earth. The essential meaning and intention for Neanderthal burial was to place the body where life originated, the interior of the earth. Neanderthal burial is therefore the earliest evidence of religion. This view of the interior of the earth as the origin of life was shared by Homo sapiens sapiens, and further contributed to the next expression of the Paleolithic earth cultus, cave art.

Chapter 4

Paleolithic Cave Art

In this chapter I will introduce the main characteristics of European cave art, followed by a discussion and critique of many of the prominent theories for the phenomenon of the cave images. I will then present my view for the meaning of the art, basing it upon a hypothesis I refer to as the "petitionary-midwife theory." Using this model I will argue that the animal and occasional plant images were engraved and painted primarily, but not exclusively, by female midwives as petitions for and assistance to the earth to bring them to life. Early humans through the subconscious perceptual processes of animism, anthropomorphism, dreams, and the conscious reasoning of analogy, perceived and conceived the earth to be a living mother that brought forth animal and plant life from the interior of her body. The cave gave access to the interior of the earth, while the narrow areas painted with red ochre symbolized menstrual blood and the birth of life. The prevalence of hand prints, footprints, colored dots, and the presence of small children and infants in the art caves suggest that the artists were primarily women. The animal image-faunal anomaly also provides support for my petitionary midwife theory.

Cave art is an expression of an earth cultus or geocentric and gynocentric religion. Cave art, like human burial, is an interaction with the earth in a meaningful way; and like intentional burial, cave art is an expression of the same religious view, that life had a beginning from the interior of the earth.

Characteristics of Cave Art

The focus of this study is European cave art. Some of the oldest European cave art was discovered in 1995 in the Chauvet cave in southeast France. Here a total of 447 painted and engraved animals, which include 14 different species have been discovered, (Harrington, 1999) some of which have been radiocarbon dated to 32,000 BP and may be older (Balter, 2000).

During the summer of 2000, what could be the oldest cave art radiocarbon dated to 36,500-32,000 BP was discovered in Fumane cave in north Italy. Five rock slabs once part of the cave surface were found fallen to the floor. Painted in red ochre, two of the images on the slabs have been identified as partial animals (Balter, 2000).

It has been estimated that there are approximately 350 sites of European Upper Paleolithic cave art dating from circa 35,000-10,000 BP (Clottes, 2001, p. 462). The art has been found from Spain to the Ural Mountains of Russia, but at least 95 percent of it is located in France and Spain (Clottes & Lewis -Williams, 1998, pp. 37, 59). A conservative estimate is that there may be between 10,000-15,000 cave art images from the Upper Paleolithic era (Pfeiffer, 1982, p. 140).

Characteristics of Paleolithic parietal or cave art include super-impositioning, use of red ochre, torches and limestone lamps for illumination, and engraving and painting of animal and plant images. Paleolithic art is found on the walls of open-air sites, that is, under overhangs of rock that served as shelters and camp sites, in the entrance of caves in living areas, further back in passageways, and in quite remote areas of usually limestone caves. The chosen areas were smooth surfaces unmarred by calcite deposition, seeping water, or cracks (Clottes & Lewis-Williams, 1998, p. 54).

Many peoples in the past have decorated shelter walls; however, the preference for decorating deep within a cave not used for habitation and not often visited is peculiar only to the Paleolithic era (Sieveking, 1997). After surveying approximately 300 caves of cave art in Western Europe, researchers estimate that approximately half of them could be classified as deep caves having art in areas of complete darkness (Bahn, 1997, p. 35). Easily accessible and suitable cave surfaces were usually ignored by the artists in favor of narrow and deep passageways where it was difficult to enter and to see the art images (Sieveking, 1997, p. 25).

The animals are usually painted or engraved in outline, generally in a static pose; they are presented with little regard for relative size, or position, that is large are associated with small, some figures are placed vertically or inverted and many are "superimposed" (p. 26) meaning, figures are often placed randomly one on top of another. At times there are so many that it is difficult to distinguish separate images.

Working in the caves required illumination. Traces of fires have been found on cave floors as well as hollowed-out slabs of limestone and sandstone that contained animal fat burned with a wick of some kind (Ucko & Rosenfeld, 1967, p. 50). More than 130 of these oil or animal-fat lamps have been found, some with the remains of juniper sprigs used as wicks (Leroi-Gourhan, 1982, pp. 75, 58). Recent experiments performed with limestone lamps found that, when animal fat and vegetable wicks were used, they could provide illumination for several hours (Vialou, 1998).

In the use of paint color, red is the oldest followed by black (Nougier, 1966, p. 590). Minerals used were iron oxides also known as red ochre, "carbon and manganese dioxide for the blacks...A few early and rare paintings were made in yellow (Lascaux, Chauvet) or white (one hand stencil at Gargas)" (Clottes & Lewis-Williams, 1998, p. 49). The use of blue and green colors have not been found (Ucko & Rosenfeld, 1967, p. 58).

The paint pigments could have been applied dry, as a paste, or liquid. While no instruments of application have been found, the paint pigments were likely applied with the fingers, animal-hair brushes, or as crayons (Bahn & Vertut, 1997, pp. 117-118). Some type of binder would have been used, such as animal fat or plant oil. Cave water also contains calcium carbonate. This could also have contributed to the bonding and the preserving of the paint pigments to the stone surfaces.

Animals were drawn without a concern for scale and generally were smaller than life-size. Animal images are constantly portrayed in profile and often seem to float or hover in space, as no ground or background is ever depicted.

Use of natural contours of the cave rock often enhances this effect. The whole animal may be represented, a head, or only the head and front legs. Many images are carefully detailed, and others appear to have been made quickly with little concern. Natural landscape is lacking; there are no rivers, mountains, rain, clouds, stars, moon, or sun (Clottes & Lewis-Williams, 1998, p. 49). The elements of human life are also absent: There is no representation of hut or tent, fire, tools, or recognizable weapons (except for the barbed signs on animals, if these indeed represent weapons). And the humans, shown naked or with so few details that it is difficult to make out any precise article of clothing, never participate in the scene (p. 48).

While engravings and paintings are found throughout the length of the caves, in the deepest areas places for the art consisted of natural features such as overhanging rocks, near wall cracks, natural reliefs, or contours. It seems that it was the act of creating these images, not seeing them that was important (Clottes & Lewis-Williams, 1998, pp. 57-58). Placing the art in the most inaccessible areas possible also implies that the act of making the images was far more important than appearance, the degree of completeness, or durability (Bahn, 1997, p. 36). There is evidence that after the animal images were made, many of the remote galleries were not revisited and were left unattended (Sieveking, 1997, p. 34).

By far the animals most portrayed in cave art are the large herbivores; horses are the most often represented animal, followed by bison and oxen, together represent 60 percent of all animal cave art. The majority of the remaining 40 percent consists of deer, ibex, and mammoth images (Sieveking, 1979, pp. 134-135). Outline engravings of animals outnumber paintings. Whether engraved or painted, perhaps as much as 90 percent of cave art consists of simple outlines (Halverson, 1992, p. 390).

Plants are also portrayed in cave art. The use of plant images in Paleolithic art has still not been adequately studied (Marshack, 1991, p. 210). What were formerly referred to as barbed signs, harpoons, or feathers by Breuil, Leroi-Gourhan (1967, p. 146) and others, have been shown by Marshack (1991) in many instances to be plants.

Painted plant images are found on and in front of a horse and in front of a bull at Lascaux. A number of painted plants are on or near a bison and a horse at Marsoulas, and a plant painted black is located near two red vulva shapes at El Castillo, Spain (pp. 173, 196, 220, 222, 319). Many engraved or etched plant images have also been found on portable art (pp. 170-174, 203, 260). There are depictions drawn in the Paleolithic caves of La Mouthe, (Gimbutus, 1989, p. 103) and Cosquer cave in France that resemble those images convincingly identified by Marshack as plants (Clottes & Courtin, 1996, pp.72, 141, 144-145).

While some of the plant images have been identified as grasses, none has been identified as edible. However, there is evidence from a hearth area dated to circa 27,000-25,000 BP, of the fleshy edible roots of aster and daisy plants (Pringle, 1998a). The remains of fossil pollen also suggest that some of the plants used as food during the Upper Paleolithic era include huckleberry, mushrooms, tubers or bulbs of the wild lily, and tender shoots of grasses (Leroi-Gourhan, 1989, p.125).

While there are regional, chronological, and style variations in the cave art, there is a unity that indicates a common and shared state of mind that remained intact for 25,000 years from circa 35,000-10,000 BP (Clottes & Lewis-Williams, 1998, p. 59). The question is: for the Paleolithic artists, what was the meaning of the animal and plant images of cave art?

Theories To Explain Cave Art

Since the find of the first cave art discovered in 1868 at Altamira, Spain, many theories have been offered to explain the intention for the art. These include decoration, hunting, fertility-magic, shamanism, stories or group myths, information exchange between groups and individuals, and psychological and dream theories. The view that the images were the result of a religious view has also been advocated.

Some researchers are pessimistic about ever finding the true intention for the existence of European cave art.

One such researcher comments that the correct interpretation for the intent of cave art is not likely to advance very far and that it is mostly a waste of time to pursue an investigation (Bahn, 1978, p. 125). Over the years, however, speculation continues in an effort to explain the intention or meaning for Upper Paleolithic cave art.

An early theory of Paleolithic art offered during the late 1800's was "art for art's sake." Its only function was to please the eye as decoration (Bahn & Vertut, 1997, p. 170). This view fell into disrepute through intervening years as other theories were advanced. Halverson (1987) has recently revived this view, claiming that the art is not a result of practical, mythical, magical, or religious intention or meaning; rather, it is due to an innate human need for artistic expression or aesthetic play, a delight in appearance. Further, this artistic activity contributed to the improvement of self-awareness and conscious reasoning and reflection (pp. 63-71).

Since Upper Paleolithic humans appreciated symmetry and appearance as evidenced in tool making, I can accept Halverson's view that the focus of attention and concentration through artistic endeavor contributed to cognitive evolution, However, while the theory of art for art's sake is a reasonable view to explain the art located at outdoor rock-shelters and at the entrance of caves, it is inadequate to account for much of the art that is located in deep caves. In about half of the caves in Western Europe, the art is located in deep caves (Bahn, 1997, pp. 35-37). Some of the areas containing engraved and painted animal images are so difficult to access and are so far back in the cave interior that it takes hours to get to the site (Marshack, 1991, p. 231). After having made the animal images, many of the remote galleries were not revisited and were left unattended (Sieveking, 1997, p. 34). It would be highly unlikely that so much time and effort would have been expended to make art for art's sake in such remote locations, never to be visited again.

A further argument against the view of art as decoration is that, due to the times of uncertainty in finding game, a hunting culture is often characterized by anxiety regarding having a successful hunt and group survival.

Thus in this environment, the notion of art for art's sake would seem incongruous (Nougier, 1966, p. 574). While early humans surely would have had time to devote to leisure, it is improbable that so much time and effort would be spent on entertainment in such inaccessible sites.

Finally, why is it, if the art were drawn for decoration and a delight in appearance that the animals are often drawn upside down in relation to the floor and are often incomplete? Also much of the art is super-impositioned, images placed one on top of another with little regard for previous works, even though plenty of suitable empty wall space is available nearby (Dickson, 1990, p. 113).

French prehistorian Henri Breuil (1979), the foremost advocate of the hunting-fertility magic theory remarked: "the daily pursuit of game and its multiplication by Nature, or the success of hunting expeditions were the principal anxieties; that the game should be plentiful, that it should increase and that sufficient should be killed, were the chief aims" (p. 23). Breuil cited examples of male animals closely following females that are in calf. He thought this was evidence of the magical reproduction of game. He also cites several examples of animals that appear to have been marked with symbolic arrows and javelins, evidence for him of hunting magic (p. 24).

A recent advocate of the hunting-magic theory, yet with an unusual approach, Waller (1993) argues that the cave art consists mainly of the images of ungulates, animals with hooves, such as horses, deer, aurochs, and bison, that are usually located in areas of higher sound reverberation in rock shelters, canyons, and chamber areas within caves. He thinks the artists chose a specific site for the art based on the acoustical quality for the purpose of imitating the sounds of running animals as part of a hunting-magic ritual. The intent for the ritual was to summon the game animals (p. 501).

A persuasive argument against the hunting-magic theory is that of Leroi-Gourhan (1982).

"Our hesitation in accepting unreservedly that animal figures were used as magic targets by hunters is because this role cannot be demonstrated, for the number of wounded animals is no more than 4% of the total number of animals represented....Why are animals marked with wounds at vital points on only a small proportion of the figures when the practice of magic would have led one to suppose that all subjects would have been marked by the mortal sign?" (p. 57, 74).

A more recent study confirmed that only about three or four percent of cave art animal images have some sort of missile on or near them (Bahn & Vertut, 1997, p. 172). Marshack (1991) argues another convincing point against the view of the cave art as an expression of hunting magic rites. Some caves with animal art are so difficult to get into and their painted and engraved chambers are so deep that hours were spent climbing inside, time was spent in engraving, painting, and ceremony, and more time was spent in coming out. This would be a tiring and uneconomic activity for a hunter performing "hunting magic." In true hunting magic, one can draw the animal in the sand or scratch it on an open rock surface and perform the rite of magic quickly (p. 231).

Eaton (1978) elaborates on the hunting-magic view: due to the accuracy of the depiction of the animal as to species, sex, age, and the emphasis on the head region, the Paleolithic art of animals found in painting and sculpture represent a group record of trophy hunting. The hunters made images of the animals that were killed in the hunt (pp. 115-116).

However, Halverson (1992) points out that the animal images of Paleolithic art do not appear to be depictions based on memory of a particular animal but, are generalized images, suggesting an ability for cognitive projection (pp. 230, 233). There is also a relative unconcern by the artists for gender differences of the animals. While there are a number of animals that can be recognized as male or female, there are many more that cannot be identified. The images depict a general species rather than particular animals from actual visual recall (p. 226). Halverson also comments on both fertility and hunting-magic theories:

"Surely it is noteworthy that among possible compositional groupings, there are no depictions whatever, I believe, of a mother animal with her young, though such a sight must have been commonplace. And in fact, if the experience and goals of the hunt were paramount in the artists' minds, young animals (as well as old and injured animals), being prime predator targets, should have been represented. But this is not the case. There are, I think, no identifiable calves, colts, or kids at all among the many thousands of depictions of bison, bovids, caprids, deer, and horses in Paleolithic art. Nor are there any depictions of identifiably maimed or dead animals" (p. 226).

There is no credible evidence to support the view that the images represent fertility magic rites. The depiction of adult animals with juveniles that one would expect for fertility magic occurs in only a couple of cases (Smith, 1992, p. 28). The only known scene of possible animal mating is at La Chaire a Calvin, and that may be a superimposition of one horse over another with no direct relationship, such superimposition being very common in cave art. After having examined this particular representation from La Chaire, (Clottes &Lewis-Williams, 1998, p.52) in my view the image does not appear to be a mating scene, as the horse said to be on top is stretched out just above and of almost equal length with the horse below. Anyone who has ever seen the reproductive act of horses would not possibly identify this as a sexual scene. The two images appear to be simply the result of superimposition.

The view that male shamans made the animal art during altered states of consciousness has become popular in recent years. This view has been advocated by Lewis-Williams & Dowson (1988) who think that Paleolithic art originated in what they refer to as "entopic phenomena." The term entoptic is derived from a Greek word meaning "within vision."

These entoptics are defined as geometric patterns that occur within the optic system including the eye and the brain, especially during altered states of consciousness.

Lewis-Williams & Dowson selected six of the most common entoptics for their study including the grid shape, parallel lines, dots or flecks, zigzag lines, and curved and meandering lines (p. 203). Evidence of these are said to be present in the art of the historic San peoples of South Africa and Coso American Indian art of California. The art is said to have been produced by shamans who entered an altered state of consciousness consisting of three stages. Based on the evidence of drug experimentation, altered states of consciousness seem to consist of stages (p. 204). The first stage consists of awareness of the entoptics, which are elaborated into familiar images during the second stage. In the third stage these are hallucinated into the images that are then portrayed in the rock art (p. 209). The African art is compared to European Paleolithic art to show similarities.

Study of the historic San Bushman and Coso peoples and their art shows use of these entoptic images incorporated into their art. According to Lewis-Williams & Dowson, these same basic visual patterns are also found in the later developed animal images of European Paleolithic art circa 35,000-10,000 BP, thereby confirming the view that the art was produced by male shamans during an altered state of consciousness. In a later study, Clottes & Lewis-Williams (1998) argue that the Paleolithic artists considered the caves to be passages leading to the underworld. (p. 99) Shamans painted the animal images during an altered state of consciousness. Clottes & Lewis-Williams characterize their view as a "dual neuropsychological and ethnographic approach," (p. 112) again relating it to the rock art of the African San peoples.

From a phenomenological point of view, the use of analogy by Clottes & Lewis-Williams is unacceptable. Bahn & Vertut (1997) give a very sound critique of this view by stating that this new approach of entoptic phenomena, shamanism, and ethnographic parallel "is based on massive assumptions, wishful thinking, and extreme selectivity of image and of interpretation." Further, none of the eyewitnesses of the San artists at work mention them as being medicine men or as being in an altered state of consciousness (pp. 182-183).

In my view, Clottes & Lewis-Williams are correct to focus on the qualitative function of human consciousness. However, as will be discussed, Paleolithic art is not the result of altered states of consciousness but rather innate cognitive processes common to early Homo sapiens sapiens, including animism, anthropomorphism, dreams, and rudimentary analogical reasoning.

In another theoretical approach, Marshack (1991) argues that much of the portable and cave art might have represented recorded calendar or "time-factored" events of life such as seasons and rituals. The images were also "storied," that is, they represent various seasonal events such as the growth of plants, the annual or daily movements of animals or of a successful hunt; and the female vulvae and Venus figures might indicate the storied function and process of reproduction. While Marshack does not impute what the content of these time-factored stories might have been, he nonetheless does "assume" (p. 283) that this is the intention for most of the Paleolithic art. Some of Marshack's view is reasonable. His evidence for a human concern with the notation of time seems convincing. However, in regard to markings on Paleolithic bone that might possibly be notations of time, (pp. 147-168) Marshack supports this interpretation by reference to similar notations by historic Australian aborigines and American Indian artifacts. Though he does warn that one should be careful of such analogies, Marshack continues to use them (p. 136).

While events surely would have been remembered, the view that most of the animal and the human images are storied is not persuasive. According to Marshack, "Every process recognized and used in human culture becomes a story...which includes characters...who change or do things in time" (p. 283). Aside from a minority of animal images and plants interpreted as seasonal, there seems to be little detail or action that would indicate some kind of story.

Many researchers have remarked on the static pose of the animals, (Sieveking, 1997, p. 26) and there is only a slight chance that there is but a single animation scene in all of Paleolithic cave art (Leroi-Gourhan, 1982, p. 38).

The presence of action and storied images do not appear until much later in time with the Mesolithic art of Cantabria in Spain.

Marshack (1991) thinks the art represents storied images of present and past, portrayed during ceremonies and rites over time as a tradition (p. 283). Any story is based on the past, that is, on memory stored. Marshack thinks the art represents a way of relating to the past through story. While I agree there is a concern with time, it is also just as possible that the art could represent a way of relating with or anticipating the future.

Based somewhat on Marshack's view, there has been an increase in support for the view that cave art represented or had some sort of information value. Barton, Clark, & Cohen (1994) think there is a temporal, spatial, and style significance in both cave and portable Upper Paleolithic art. They see these characteristics as performing an important social function of information exchange (p. 151). Barton et al. make a distinction between portable art, mostly ornaments, which carries information about the individual to other individuals, and cave art which transmits information from group to group (p. 187). They see cave art as beginning during the time of Upper Paleolithic population increase. With more individuals and larger groups competing for resources, land, and food, the need for communication increased. Cave art developed as demarcations or physical landmarks that served to define group territorial boundaries. The various styles of art served to further identify group claims and reduce intergroup conflict. These claims were symbolically expressed through art, especially since it modified the landscape. The art thus contributed to an overall social organization (pp. 200-201).

While information was surely exchanged and competition for resources and territorial boundaries would have existed among Upper Paleolithic groups, Barton's et al. view would not satisfactorily explain the intention for many of the animal images. For if the images served as markers, why not place most of this art outside of caves or at least within the entry areas? More than 50 percent of the art is located in deep passageways and once drawn was seldom revisited (Sieveking, 1997).

Mithen (1988) advocates another variation of the theory that the art represents an exchange of information. Considering both cave and portable art, Mithen presents examples of various Paleolithic images that he refers to as animal signs including tracks, defecation, resting or rolling on the ground, evidence of eating vegetation, and auditory images of calling or moving. After hunters located game in the environment, they drew detailed observations of the animals as storied indications of a future potential. The images indicate a theme of information gathering. Mithen (1988) defines information as "knowledge about the location and state of potential resources" (p. 297). To support his view, he presents images from contemporary hunting-gathering groups. The art images focused attention on these particular aspects of animal behavior, such as posture and activities that served to provide mnemonic cues utilized by the teacher artists to educate young hunters in the active search for game animals.

I disagree with Mithen's assumption that portable art and parietal or cave art have the same meaning. The "greatest proliferation" of portable occurred circa 15,000-12,000 BP (Mellars, 1998, p. 68) and the intention for much of it was decorative. Except for the sculpted female figures, the intention for portable art was not religious; while cave art and the female figures, as I shall seek to establish, has a religious intention. Second, like many researchers, Mithen uses the analogy of historically studied groups to support his view. As previously mentioned, in my view the use of analogy produces unacceptable interpretations.

Pfeiffer (1983) also thinks the art represented information and began as a result of evolving intelligence and a population increase and formation of larger groups of 100-200 individuals. This increase in population brought with it more complexity and conflict as well as an information explosion. Prior to the development of cave art, experienced events were stored in memory. But with an increase in information, events began to be stored through visual images. The young were then initiated into this evolving knowledge through the ordeal of getting to the art, at times as deep as one-third of a mile into the earth's interior.

The art was a "tribal encyclopedia" (p. 41) of myths whose content is unknown. However, Pfeiffer speculates that the myths expressed a concern with religious morals and heroes and villains through the use of music, song, and dance, with art providing the background scenes. He supports his view by comparison to the customs of contemporary hunting-gathering groups, such as the Australian aborigines. This view of the intention for the art is highly speculative and is again based on historical comparisons, for which there is no evidence during the Paleolithic era.

In yet another version of the art as information or communication, Hayden (1993) points out that Upper Paleolithic culture was a hunting-gathering lifestyle. With a population increase came organization and the ability to exploit natural resources. Task specialization developed such as leaders, skilled processors of large-scale animal kills, and artists who entered the caves to depict the animal images. Art did not flourish until the late half of the Upper Paleolithic era when population density and the ability for resource exploitation dramatically increased (p. 138). The cave paintings were used as "ritual and corporate showpieces" of status, the primary purpose of which was to attract and impress people who then contributed to the economic power and success of the group who sponsored the artists (p. 130). Hayden thinks that cave art was related to status display involving competing groups. He thinks the images depicted either totemic animals of a particular group, group myths, or even the animal allies of shamans during visionary experiences of initiations into these groups (p. 138).

While increasing population could have influenced the increase of the art during the late Paleolithic era, I cannot agree that it was the intention for the art. The making of the art began circa 35,000 BP and endured until the late half of the Upper Paleolithic era that Hayden mentions, circa 14,000 BP, and was no longer produced by the end of this time circa 10,000 BP.

During much of the Paleolithic era Homo sapiens sapiens population group size approximated that of Neanderthals, about an average of 25 individuals (Hyland, 1993, pp. 707-710). Hayden's view also appears to have been influenced by his study of the dynamics of historic tribal groups, and therefore this cannot be reliably applied to Paleolithic culture, especially since there is no artifact evidence to support this view.

Collins & Onian (1978) argue a psychoanalytic view of the intention for the cave art, that it was the result of the frustration of adolescent males, prevented from hunting big game and kept away from women by the adult males. Their frustration contributed to the production of the images of their desire, vulvas, the female body, and animals to be hunted. The young males projected their fantasies of sex and hunting onto the artistic images, which provided substitute visual and tactile satisfaction (p. 21). This unusual view appears to be based solely on the study of historical tribal groups and Freudian psychology. There is no credible archeological evidence to support this view.

Dreaming could also have served as a cognitive influence for making art. Van de Castle (1994) argues that, since early humans spent a fair amount of time interacting with animals, chasing or being chased, and experiencing associated emotions such as awe or fear, images of animals would have appeared frequently in dreams. These images were then communicated to others of the group by etching or painting them on the cave surfaces (pp. 46-47). I agree with Van de Castle that dreams contributed to the cognitive inspiration for the art and that the intention for the images was communication; I disagree that the intention for the images was communication to other humans. This view cannot satisfactorily explain why if communication was intended, the artists placed over half of the artwork in difficult-to-reach areas of the cave that were seldom visited.

Leroi-Gourhan's (1967, pp. 172-175) influential view rejected the hunting-magic theory. He conceived that the intention for the art was a religious interest on the part of the artists for that which brought life into existence; namely, both male and female genders.

This interest, he thought, was expressed by the placement of what he classified as male signs and male animals, such as the horse, in the outer cave areas or panels and by placing what he classified as female signs and animals, such as the bison, in the central area or panels of the cave.

This intentional patterned arrangement of animals by the artists formed a meaningful structure, what he referred to as a "mythogram." However, in his last published work, Leroi-Gourhan relinquished the classification of animals into male and female categories; yet he still saw some significance in the groupings of the animals concluding that the cave was probably symbolic of a female womb and that the artists had practiced some sort of fertility cult in using magical rites (Leroi-Gourhan, 1982, pp. 58-62).

A convincing contrary argument is that the artists often used the contours and the surface shapes in the caves so that these natural features imposed the depiction of a particular animal (Clottes & Lewis-Williams, 1998, pp. 56-57; Lorblanchet, 1989, p. 110). The caves seem to have been decorated at random, and each animal image appears to have had an individual and an isolated importance (Sieveking, 1997, p. 27). For Conkey (1984) Leroi-Gourhan's theory is a monolithic interpretation that assumes inaccurately that the artists had the ability for modern modes of philosophical thought (p. 259).

Some scholars are skeptical of finding any meaning or intention for Paleolithic cave art (Davidson, 1997, p. 128). Other researchers think that any single or monolithic meaning for the art is not creditable (Lewis-Williams, 1997, pp. 321, 324). Since the cave art is an expression of varying rituals conducted in some 350 caves over thousands of years, there is no reason to expect that all of the art had a single ritual intention or purpose (Shreeve, 1995, pp. 314-315).

Breuil and Leroi-Gourhan, two of the most influential interpreters of the art, proposed that a single and major cultural intention or meaning did serve to generate the art (Conkey, 1983, p. 204).

While Breuil thought the single meaning was hunting and fertility magic, Leroi-Gourhan held the view that the art was the intention of some sort of a religious fertility cult.

My research findings show that there was a single meaning and intention for the phenomenon of Paleolithic cave art over a span of 25,000 years, and that as Leroi-Gourhan and a few other investigators insist, it was the result of a religious view.

Rappaport (1999) comments, "Art and religion seem ancient or even primordial companions...the most plausible attempts to explain art's origins are those taking it to emerge from or with religion" (pp. 384-385). Laming (1959) relates the cave images to religion, advocating that the art expressed a relationship with a primal monotheistic Creator and that the placing of the representations within the caves had a religious significance (pp. 166-167).

Lorblanchet (1989) argues that the cave art was an artistic process of relating the animal images with or to the "universal forces of creation" (p. 139). While each of these researchers comment only briefly and offer no further specific evidence, I agree with Rappaport's, Laming's, and Lorblanchet's views here, and propose that the essential meaning of the cave art is what I refer to as the "petitionary-midwife theory."

Petitionary-Midwife Theory

I have thoroughly researched the artifact evidence of Paleolithic cave art and numerous theories that seek to explain the meaning and intention for the phenomenon. By focusing attention on Paleolithic cave art, and suspending association, analogical reasoning, and comparison with what is known of historic tribal art, I reached the following conclusions that I refer to as the petitionary-midwife model:

1. Upper Paleolithic cave art is an interaction with the earth in a meaningful way.

2. The cognitive basis for this behavioral interaction was the animistic perception of the earth as a living entity, and the anthropomorphic perception and analogical conception that the interior of the earth was a female place of origin.
3. The animal and occasional plant images were petitions directed to the earth as the origin of animal and plant life to provide food.
4. The cave artists were predominantly women and to a much lesser extent gynocentrically oriented males, who by drawing the images based on sensory observation or dream images, acted as midwives in petitioning and assisting the earth to give birth.
5. Like burial, cave art is an expression of an earth cultus or geocentric and gynocentric religion.

These main points summarize the structure of the petitionary-midwife model. I will establish that the animal images were engraved and painted primarily but not exclusively, by female midwives as petitions and assistance to the earth to bring forth life. Through animism, anthropomorphism, dreams, and conscious rudimentary reasoning, humans perceived and conceived the earth to be a living female that brought forth living forms from the interior of her body. The cave gave access to the greater interior of the earth, while the narrow areas coated with red ochre symbolized menstrual blood and the coming into existence of life. Evidence of animal bones placed in the floor, cracks, and fissures of cave walls at about a dozen French sites including Enlene, Les Trois-Freres, and Gargas, also suggests an assistance to the earth to bring forth life. The prevalence of hand prints, footprints, colored dots, and the presence of small children and infants in the French art caves of Gargas, Pech Merle, Bedeilhac, Chauvet, and others, suggest the artists were primarily women assisted by gynocentrically oriented males. The phenomenon of the animal image-faunal anomaly also provides support for the petitionary midwife theory. Cave art is an expression of an earth cultus or geocentric and gynocentric religion.

To present the essential structure of the petitionary-midwife model, it is necessary to examine the beginning of Upper Paleolithic cave art.

The overall evidence supports the view that an evolving intelligence had to reach a level of cognitive ability before artistic creativity could be expressed. For thousands of years, human cognitive ability evolved to make various kinds of stone and wooden tools, shelters, and, though no evidence exists, probably some kind of clothing. The acquired skills of observing, shaping, and imitating developed by both Neanderthals and Homo sapiens sapiens contributed finally to cave art produced by modern humans beginning circa 35,000 BP.

A few researchers trace the beginning of cave art to the Neanderthals. Pfeiffer (1982) argues that the key to Upper Paleolithic art can be found in the earliest burial customs of the Neanderthals. Neanderthal burials evidence a set of structured views that reflect organized patterns of ritual behavior, and indicate an advancement in human intelligence that found its fullest expression in the art of Homo sapiens sapiens, circa 35,000-10,000 BP (p. 102). Other researchers also trace the beginning of art to Neanderthal behavior and artifacts:

"Interestingly the use of colouring matter and the simple carving of stone and bone (lines, cupmarks, etc.) begin before true recognizable representations, not in the Upper Palaeolithic at all but in the Mousterian. Ochre crayons are quite often found...both red and black, and several cases of carving (a cross, pairs of cup marks, etc.) are known; the first burials occur at the same time. In other words, the first drawing indications of art actively appear with...the Neanderthals, and in almost the same areas as the first representational art" (Collins & Onians, 1978, pp. 19-20).

In Spain at the Nerja caves and the El Castillo cave, researchers have found possible evidence of Neanderthal cave painting. In 2012 at the Nerja cave near Malaga Spain in an area where to date no artifact remains of Homo sapiens sapiens have been uncovered, (SciTech Daily, 2012) were found six images of seals painted with red ochre (MacErlean, 2012). That Neanderthals did consume seals is confirmed by the remains of animals including seals, dolphins, fish, and shellfish found in two caves inhabited by them on the coast of southern Spain (Roach, 2008).

Charcoal near the Nerja paintings was dated using radiocarbon dating to 43,500-42,300 BP (MacErlean, 2012). While scholars in the field have previously thought that only Homo sapiens sapiens painted images in the Paleolithic caves, a growing number of researchers accept the view, based partially on the extreme age of the art, that Neanderthals painted the images in Nerja cave.

At the El Castillo cave, dating of the paintings using uranium series dating of the calcium carbonate deposits covering the art yielded a minimum date of 40,800 BP. For some researchers the early date for the art begs the question as to whether some of the paintings could have made by Neanderthals. The paintings include red dots and negative handprints made by placing the hand on the wall surface and blowing or spiting red ochre paint around it to leave an outline of the hand. Other painted animals include bison and horses (Than, 2012).

The present generally accepted theory is that modern humans or Homo sapiens sapiens originated in southeast Africa circa 100,000 BP and perhaps earlier. D'Errico, Henshilwood, & Nilssen (2001) report on recent finds of an incised bone at the Blombos cave site in South Africa. Also discovered at the site were two shaped pieces of red ochre engraved with cross-hatched geometric designs that date to circa 77,000 BP (Henshilwood et al, 2002). The finds suggest an aptitude for and an early appreciation for geometric form by early Homo sapiens sapiens who eventually migrated into the Middle East and from there into Europe circa 40,000 BP.

However, prior to this time there exists no evidence of cave art and only isolated and sporadic expressions of portable art made by modern humans in Africa or the Middle East (Speth & Tchernov, 1998, p. 224). Consistent expression of representational art appears for the first time in Europe.

A few investigators point out that after early Homo sapiens sapiens arrived in Europe, they might have been inspired to make cave art by examining and imitating the scratching and honing of claws by bears on the softer areas of cave walls.

Study of the oldest engravings of clay and stone show random wavy lines, sometimes called "macaronis" and contour outlines, in seeming imitation of the bear markings (Maringer & Bandi, 1953, pp. 95-96; Nougier, 1966, p. 575). There were other characteristics about bears that would have interested early humans. Due to their size and strength, bears were naturally avoided as much as possible. Humans would also have competed with bears for use of lower elevation caves as shelters. The hibernation behavior of bears would also have been of interest: appearing lethargic and even temporarily dead during the winter months, and seemingly coming back to life in early spring.

I expand Maringer & Bandi and Nougier's view by suggesting that when examining the scratch marks made on the walls by bears, humans paid attention to and perceived cave animal shapes in the formations of the cave surfaces. This examination contributed to the artist's innate animistic tendency to use bulges, projections, or features in the rock and incorporate them into the animal images. "The lighting techniques used at the time, torches or grease lamps...would cast a dim and fluctuating light...When such conditions are replicated, or even when visiting a cave with a candle, the walls seem to come alive with the moving shadows cast by the flickering flame. It becomes very easy then to see animals in the shape of the rocks...perhaps shapes seen in this way were taken for real and the artists then drew animals exactly where they happened to see them, possibly bringing them to life" (Clottes, 1997, p. 211).

Other researchers have noted the use of the natural features of rocks and caves, commenting that the beginning of art may be found in the human mind (Gombrich, 1977, p. 90). "Could it not be that bulls and horses were first "discovered"...in these mysterious haunts before they were fixed and made visible to others by means of coloured earth?... What we know of the beginnings of image-making confirms the continuous link between finding and making" (p. 91, 93).

I characterize as animism the deliberate finding of the likenesses of animals and the incorporation of these natural cave features into the animal images, and the innate attributing of life to nonliving forms.

Early humans observed that living plants came from the interior of the earth and that animals were born within dens and in a sense came from the earth. Through rudimentary comprehension they understood that life came only from life, not from what was dead. Finding the rough resemblance of an animal in a cave wall, and having a basic understanding that life can come only from life and not from something that is not animated or that is dead, early humans perceived the earth as living.

There are numerous examples of the incorporation of natural cave features into the animal images. While conducting field research during March 2001, at the cave of Pech Merle located in the Lot region of central France, I observed several examples. One of the better known paintings of cave art is the frieze of dotted horses at Pech Merle. On a smooth slightly concave projected area of the cave wall located at ground level and roughly measuring one and one-half meters high and six meters in length, are a number of superimposed painted images. At the right end of the projected rock mass is a natural feature that closely resembles the head of a horse. The artist intentionally chose to add to this feature to produce the enhanced likeness of a horse measuring near five feet in length and approximately three feet in height.

The animistic perception of animal shapes in stone was also complimented by the innate perceptual process of anthropomorphism. Mithen (1997) sees conclusive evidence of anthropomorphism in statuettes and paintings of figures with both animal and human characteristics dating from circa 30,000 BP (p. 718). These figures are “anthromorphs,” animal images that appear to have some human characteristics, such as standing upright.

In what follows I will present artifact evidence that suggests that in addition to animistically perceiving the earth as alive, early humans anthropomorphically perceived it to be the womb of a greater female body that brought forth life, the evidence of which for early humans was perceived in the partial shapes of the cave surface that resembled animals.

The artists sought to assist this perceived process of birth from the interior of the earth by artistically enhancing natural inchoate images found in the rock surface of the cave.

Dream perceptions also undoubtedly served as a cognitive influence for making art. Since "dream and art, in all its varieties, are manifestations of the same biological need to convert experience into structure," (States, 1997, p. 1) it is likely that images perceived in dreams during the night were recalled upon awakening and contributed to the conscious representation of cave art. Dreams are an innate subconscious cognitive function that would have influenced prehistoric peoples.

Dreams occur during sleep without any conscious intention, nor can dreams be prevented from occurring. Most mammals have been observed to experience REM sleep, which is strongly associated with vivid dreaming. Sleep researchers have concluded that dreams had some sort of evolutionary value. Research suggests that dreams function to process experiences learned during waking hours. The view of experimental psychologists is that "dreaming serves to promote the general adaptation of people to their environment, helping them to organize their perceptions...and to connect and integrate new experiences with past memories" (Bulkeley, 1997, pp. 65, 84). Whether dreams are the result of wish fulfillment, existential situations, precognition, or the random residue of daytime events, the phenomenon of distinct black and white or color images of the dreaming process would have influenced the lives of early humans.
Rudimentary analogical reasoning also contributed to conceiving the interior of the earth to be the womb of a greater female body that brought forth life. Reasoning by analogy consists of an association of relating this with that. It is suggested by imitation in tool making by Homo erectus, Neanderthals, and Homo sapiens sapiens, that early humans possessed an ability to recognize similarity. This ability would have necessitated a learned set of purposeful behaviors and ability to plan and a talent for imitation in making one tool like another, suggesting a developing ability for rudimentary analogical reasoning as well.

Klein (1990) argues that an actual change in brain function occurred circa 47,000-38,000 BP which brought about an increased ability for analogical reasoning. He sees evidence for this in the rapid expansion of Upper Paleolithic culture, and an improvement in the lithic technology during this time.

The cognitive perceptual processes of animism and anthropomorphism, the vivid dream images and rudimentary analogical reasoning contributed to the development of a geocentric and gynocentric orientation to existence.

Geocentrism and Gynocentrism

Paleolithic cave art is the result of human intention and expression; yet in all of the engraved and painted depictions, there are no images of human presence such as a hut, fire, recognizable tools, or realistic weapons. Moreover, humans are never shown as participating in a scene or wearing any recognizable clothing (Clottes & Lewis-Williams, 1998, pp. 48-49). Parietal art could therefore be comprehended to have no direct relevance to hunting, fertility, action stories, or information directed to humans. Theories for cave art based on these views appear to be the result of modern anthropocentrism, considering humans to be more important than other living or nonliving forms.

Occasionally an engraved or painted vulva (Marshack, 1991, p. 318; Giedion, 1962, p. 191) or an engraved shaped outline of the female form (Ucko & Rosenfeld, 1967, pp. 210-211; Breuil, 1979, pp. 334-335) is found in the cave art but there are no scenes of human activity. Some researchers refer to the presence of a few engraved or painted male “sorcerers” in the art, but as the next chapter explains these depictions are more accurately attributed to super-impositioning, anthropomorphized animals, or creative imagination.

The engraved and the painted images of living forms located on the surfaces of caves and some rock-shelters consist almost exclusively of animals and some plants.

The phenomenon of cave art consists of a focus of human attention directed primarily to the earth, and then to the relationship of animals and plants with the earth. Human activity is not depicted, suggesting that humans are subordinate to the earth and animals and plants. The evidence suggests that early humans had a pronounced geocentric orientation to existence.

If the intention of cave art is to be correctly comprehended, investigation requires more of a geocentric emphasis. Tattersall (1998) thinks there can be little question that whatever view or myth the Upper Paleolithic art represented, "it incorporated at least implicitly the notion that these people were themselves an integral component of their natural habitat, which was thus a greater entity than they" (p. 217). Evidence supports this geocentric view. The evidence of cave art suggests that humans recognized living forms to have an origin from the interior of the earth, accessed via the awesome presence of caves.

In general, the modern attitude toward caves is that they are alien and frightening places, inhabited by snakes, insects, spiders, bats, and possibly even a bear. However, for early humans, caves were much more than just holes in the ground. Caves and many large rock-ledge overhangs served as shelters and protection from excessive heat or cold, rain, and snow storms. During the Paleolithic era as today, caves probably averaged between 50-55 degrees Fahrenheit as a constant year round temperature.

The entrances of caves were sometimes used as living areas. Through pollen analysis, evidence indicates that in some caves used during the Upper Paleolithic era, large amounts of summer grasses and flowers were brought into the caves, probably for sleeping and for warmth (Bahn & Vertut, 1997, p. 12). Almost all footprints found in French Paleolithic caves belong to children, indicating a lack of fear of this subterranean environment (Bahn, 1997, p. 36). Interestingly, of any of the Upper Paleolithic art caves, no human skeletal remains have ever been found in the depths of the caverns (Pfeiffer, 1982, p. 126).

While Upper Paleolithic humans would have experienced geographic sites such as a canyon, high cliff, mountain, large river, waterfall, or ocean, as mysterious or unusual, the cave environment may have been the most extraordinary. Unusually dark, and quiet, often containing lengthy passageways and large chambers, having a constant temperature, and sheltering various animals, the cave interior would have been in sharp contrast to the environment above. In the caves in the French Pyrenees, the entrances to some are so impressive as to evoke the experience of a passage or transition into another world (Clottes & Lewis-Williams, 1998, p. 81). Having traveled to France during March 2001, and having viewed the entrances to both Niaux and Bedeilhac caves located in the Pyrenees, I would agree with Clottes & Lewis-Williams. By my estimate the entrance of the Bedeilhac cave measures roughly 45 meters wide and 22 meters high, and the opening of Niaux is nearly the same.

Visiting the grottos of Gargas, Pech Merle, and Bedeilhac, I found the interiors of these caves are no less awe inspiring. Within these caves are springs that percolate and continuously flow and drip from the ceilings, walls, and floors; there are projections and bulges everywhere that include elongated and odd speleogen or erosion formed pendent and flowstone shapes that suggest coming into existence. The caves contain various speleotherms or mineral water depositions and concretions such as conical stalactites and stalagmites, columns, roof crust, helictites, fistula, wavy and folded curtains, cave coral, and cave pearls. There are various cavities such as chambers, rooms, domes, vaults, passages, fissures, and small and large dripholes. The overall impression of the unusual projections and elongated flowing shapes and areas of the cave environment strongly suggest a place of shaping, forming, or of coming into existence.

My view is that the interior of the earth was perceived to be the origin of existence. In modern times, one cannot help but sense the life energy in the growth of plants and trees in the spring of the year. Early humans most likely attributed this bursting forth of energy in plants and in the young of burrowing insects and animals, and the hibernating bears coming forth from their dens, as originating from or given birth to by the earth.

Life came not from what was above the earth or from a visible or invisible beyond but rather from within. Upper Paleolithic humans palpably sensed the below to be the origin of the visible world above.

Migratory flocks of birds, salmon runs, migrating reindeer, horses, bison, and cattle, were understood to have arrived from and departed to some place distant. Yet this distant place was likely not conceived as on the earth in terms of a vast distance of hundreds or even thousands of miles away, but rather identified as a not too distant and findable place within the earth. The large flocks, schools of fish, and herds of animals such as horses and reindeer would have not been understood as a migration, but almost as if they were coming from and or returning to an origin, which was not the vast surface expanse but rather the interior of the earth. While he does not offer details, Geist (1978) also thinks that during the Paleolithic era the caves were perceived as the origin of the animals (p. 322).

Out of the darkness of night came the sun, moon, planets, stars, and comets. To early humans, these heavenly bodies would have appeared to literally rise from within the earth as they appeared on the horizon. All were likely to have been perceived as daily arising from and descending back into the interior darkness of some greater opening of the earth beyond the distant horizon.

When darkness came, so did sleep, which resembles death; from the darkness of sleep came dreams, night visions. Since dreaming usually occurred during the darkness of night, sleep and dream images would have also been associated with the ever-darkness of the cave.

The caves could have been animistically perceived to give birth to the springs and streams usually found within them. Thermal springs that did not freeze would have been perceived as especially significant. It is possible to speculate that since mammals are warm to the touch, and that a lack of bodily heat is associated with death, that this observation could have further contributed to the animistic perception that the warmth of the hot springs coming from below was from a living entity and was therefore the place of origin of living things.

It has been observed that a significant number of caves and sites containing cave art in France are in very close proximity to springs, and especially thermal/mineral springs (Bahn & Vertut, 1997, p. 200).

For early humans, caves would have been the answer to the question of where all living things came from. Having observed human life come from the smaller opening of the womb for thousands of years, it would have been natural to first animistically, anthropomorphically, and during dreaming, to perceive and then analogically equate where all things came from to the larger cave openings and interior of the earth. Both human and animal life came from within the dark unseen interior of the mother to exit into the visible exterior world. Caves were the greater interior which humans could experience, and as the evidence suggests, was understood to be female or feminine. The human female was the origin of life and also provided the nourishment of breast milk, both characteristics which represent the two great commandments of biological existence, to eat and to reproduce. Paleolithic hunting-gathering groups, observing that many living forms came from or lived in the soil or rocks, would have perceived the earth as likened to the greater female origin or mother from which life had a beginning and who also provided nourishment for their own life existence.

Leroi-Gourhan (1967) comments, "The cave as a whole does seem to have had a female symbolic character, which would explain the care with which narrow passages, oval-shaped areas, and the smaller cavities are marked in red, even sometimes painted entirely in red" (p. 174). This statement suggests that the oval and smaller areas and passages were perceived as the female vulva and womb, and that the painting of red ochre represented the life force of menstrual blood.

In Leroi-Gourhan's (1982) last published work, he concluded that the meaning and intention for the art was that the cave was probably symbolic of a female womb and that the artists had practiced some sort of fertility cult using magic rites (pp. 58-62). However he offered no elaboration of this view.

My view is that, rather than practicing fertility magic, early humans through the innate perceptual processes of animism, anthropomorphism, dreaming, and rudimentary analogical reasoning were practicing religion by relating the opening and interior of the female vulva to the greater opening of the cave and the interior of the earth. This view is further supported by the following comments and evidence.

"In the so-called Hall of the little Bison at Font de Gaume, so narrow a cleft that two people can hardly stand there at the same time, the wall was smeared over with red ochre before any paintings were done; and in a side recess at Altimira, and another at Gargas, the walls remain rubbed all over with red ochre only. Since this pigment was often painted on the bones of the dead and seems to have symbolized life, blood or fire...the painting of cave recesses with red ochre would appear to mean the magic making of life deep in the earth, as though in the menstruous womb of a woman" (LaBarre, 1970, p. 395).

At a number of cave sites, including the Cougnac cave of Quercy, France, natural formations of small clefts and cavities resemble a vulva shape, and have been "stained...with red ochre to symbolize the menstrual flow" (Rudgley, 1999, p. 196).

Nougier 1966) poses an important question, and then gives the most probable explanation for the existence of Paleolithic cave art:

"The figures of the Great Ceiling at Rouffignac...form an indescribable accumulation of reality pictures heaped upon one another in apocalyptic excess and disorder...all running in different directions. Why is this ceiling, this section of the cave, so wealthy in figures? It is some 870 yd. from the entrance and is preceded and followed by hundreds, perhaps thousands, of square yards of surface as regular or more so, and often more conveniently placed for painting...The choice of the ceiling...sheds light on one of the major meanings of prehistoric art, one of the underlying reasons, indeed, for its existence.

The smooth surfaces of the Great Ceiling were chosen because they spread over the largest subterranean chasm of Rouffignac, a vast funnel that gives access to the second subterranean level. The mammoths and horses, then, were conceived as escaping from the depths...This passage into the bowels of the earth is, par excellence, the sacred place of the cave...in the depths of the earth, the Earth Mother, creator, creator of men and beasts, creator of life...numerous animal figures unmistakably associated with shadowy galleries, fissures, openings of narrow passages, all kinds of 'pockets of darkness.' It has been suggested that these dark recesses were...traps or pits, into which the animal would fall and some examples can indeed be given of horses and hinds appearing to fall. But far more numerous are the animals that issue from pits, springing from dark recesses. It is thus necessary to formulate an inverse explanation: these animals rise from the bowels of the earth, the Earth Mother, creator of life and of game" (p. 586).

The evidence suggests that the artists animistically and anthropomorphically perceived the cave to be the place of the beginning of life, the womb of the earth as mother. The artist's likely intention for penetrating so deeply into the caves is that they sought to reach that greater mysterious place of the beginning of all existence.

Just as there was a mysterious place within woman, beyond the opening of her vagina, in the midst of the darkness of her abdomen or body from which a child developed and was born, so there was conceived a place deep within the interior darkness of the earth where all living things were animated and from which they came forth into life existence.

Other researchers have noticed the phenomenon of the cave art being frequently placed near the entrance to chasms or holes that lead to the mysterious and dark cave depths (Bhan & Vertut, 1997, p. 200). In the Les Eyzies region of France, there are several thousand caves and yet only about 100 of them contain cave art (Pfeiffer, 1982, p. 118). It may be of benefit to research these sites in the future to see that of those that do contain art, which of them have images placed near chasms.

The artifact evidence of the use of red ochre further suggests a gynocentric view. Ochre is a rather common mineral found in regions where caves are generally located (Leroi-Gourhan, 1957, p. 110). Of all the minerals utilized decoratively in painting, red ochre is the oldest and most frequently used (Nougier, 1966, p. 590).

In my view the use of red ochre in the Paleolithic caves had a symbolic significance. The Paleolithic people's anthropomorphic perception and rudimentary analogical conception served to associate the deposits of red ochre with blood, and especially menstrual blood. Menstrual blood was likely considered the mysterious life force of the female body from which the individual newborn appeared, covered with blood. As used in the painting of cave animal images, the ochre as a symbol of blood would also have been useful in assisting the depiction to be born or to be sent into existence. Likewise, the coating of various animal teeth and bones was most likely based on an association with the blood of birth and of life.

In about a dozen French caves, including those of Enlene and Les Trois-Freres, an important though usually over-looked feature of Paleolithic cave art has been found. Hundreds of small pieces of bone and teeth have been found placed vertically into the cave floor and the fissures and cracks of the wall. Having been determined to have served no known utilitarian purpose, some of these bones and teeth were found located near "small smudges of red paint" or "reliefs covered in red paint."

These bone fragments were transported far back into the cave and inserted into the walls for a ritual purpose (Clottes & Lewis-Williams, 1998, p. 83). This phenomenon has also been reported at Gargas cave where many animal bone fragments recently dated to 26,860 BP were found placed in a crack beside hand prints (Clottes, 1998, p. 46).

In my view, the placing of the bones was the religious act of a midwife to assist the earth to bring forth a living animal.

The gesture of placing the bone pieces and teeth in the floor and wall crevices near the red ochre smudges and reliefs that are most likely symbolic of blood, was like the engraved and painted animal images, a petition to the earth to bring forth by adding life and completed form to the part of the animal.

Recently, close attention has also been directed to what was previously regarded as random engraved marks on many of the cave walls. Most researchers of cave art have ignored these seemingly stray cut-marks in the rock as inconsequential. These cut-marks were possibly, "made into the rocky membrane to allow the escape of supernatural power and animals or to achieve some sort of relationship between the maker and the underworld that was believed to exist behind the surface, a relationship that we do not now understand...these cuts were a way of treating the underground surfaces that was different from, yet complementary to, the making of images" (Clottes & Lewis-Williams, 1998, pp. 108-109).

While speculative, the theory posits an intention and meaning for these cut-marks; they could have been made to release or to assist the life force to come forth from beneath the surface, within the earth, then perceived as the origin of living animals and plants. Many researchers have commented on the tendency of the artists to incorporate natural features of the cave surface into the image of the animal (Conkey, 1981).

"The lighting techniques used at the time, torches or grease lamps...would cast a dim and fluctuating light....When such conditions are replicated, or even when visiting a cave with a candle, the walls seem to come alive with the moving shadows cast by the flickering flame. It becomes very easy then to see animals in the shape of the rocks...perhaps shapes seen in this way were taken for real and the artists then drew animals exactly where they happened to see them, possibly bringing them to life" (Clottes, 1997, p. 211).

While he does not mention specific cognitive functions, Clottes' comment provides further support for the view of animistic and anthropomorphic perception by the artists.

In my view, the making of the cave art was a way of assisting the earth to bring forth the potential and inchoate form present in the rock surface. Petitioning the earth to give birth to or send the animals and occasional plants portrayed, and assisting in bringing them to life, is the essence of the intention for the engraving and painting of the cave images.

Clottes & Courtin (1996) suggest that the "common heritage in all of the painted caves" was that they were a sanctuary, defined as, "a place of importance with limited access where only certain people came, perhaps on special occasions, to take part in ceremonies (this term being understood in its widest sense as any activity of a cultural nature having nothing to do with the immediate physical necessities of existence)" (pp. 179-180). While I agree that the painted and engraved caves were sites accessed by only a few individual artists on special ritual occasions important to the cultural group, I disagree with the view that this activity had nothing to do with the physical necessities of existence. The animal images represent the physical desire and need for food, and are thus petitions to the earth by artist midwives to bring forth or give birth to them so they could be hunted, killed, and consumed.

A few researchers have speculated that the images of cave art were an early form of writing or that they expressed some sort of message or communication. Shortly before his death, Leroi-Gourhan remarked in regard to the cave art at Lascaux that at this site he believed the artists had come very close to developing an alphabet (Rudgley, 1999, p. 77). In my view, what he meant by this brief remark was that the artists intended some sort of communication by painting and engraving the animal images. This view and the following statement appear to be cogent observations regarding Paleolithic cave images.

"It is a fair assumption that in the last Ice Age most of the cave art contained a 'message' which was not aimed at us, and which we cannot understand...Palaeolithic art...certainly comprises a 'vocabulary' of symbols, some of which must have had considerable information value" (Bahn & Vertut, 1997, pp. 208-209).

Rather than an alphabet, the images are more accurately a mental representation of desire or entreaty. In my view, the message of the cave art vocabulary does not in any way appear to be a communication to humans, but rather portrays communication from humans to the earth. The engraving and painting of the animal images was a petition by artist midwives for the image to come into existence, or be sent, so it could be hunted or harvested. The biological necessity and desire to eat was expressed in the engraved and painted ideational images inserted onto the cave surfaces. The many animal and occasional plant images portrayed in cave art indicate the need for food. While the representation of animals is not unique throughout human existence, in general it is probably true as Collins & Onians (1978) remark, that no other culture has given their food animals such an important status in art (pp. 11, 14-15). The animal images are the expression of the desire and need for food, petitions to the earth by artist midwives to bring forth or give birth to them.

While it is often argued that the animal images are the work of hunters or shamans performing hunting magic, there is no convincing evidence for this assertion. Only three or four percent of cave art animal images have some sort of missile on or near them (Leroi-Gourhan, 1982, pp. 57, 74; Bahn & Vertut, 1997, p. 172). My findings, as will be discussed in more detail, suggest that the only images convincingly said to have weapons associated with them, occur only after 13,000 BP, near the end of the making of cave art.

Dickson (1990) speculates that the intention for cave art was that it might have been the result of "…a perceived cyclicality in the passage of time and...the periodicity and fecundity of women, were generalized into universal principles or 'grand analogies,' that formed the basis of speculation and thought about nature, humankind, the universe, and reality. This model of social and material reality was embodied and reflected in the great parietal art caves of Franco-Cantabria" (p. 215).

I agree there is an emphasis on time. The cave art images represent a concern for a time in the future when the fecundity of the earth would give birth to and send the petitioned for animals.

For Paleolithic humans the interior of the earth was a "universal principle" that was animistically, anthropomorphically, and through dreaming, perceived and then analogically conceived to be the female womb of all living and material forms.

Breuil thought that each animal image had an individual and isolated importance (Sieveking, 1997, p. 27). Other researchers have also advocated this view, "the location of many paleolithic paintings in the dark and inaccessible depths of caves, and the fact that such paintings were sometimes executed one on top of the other...strongly suggests that the act of painting them was of greater significance than the paintings themselves...and that in making them artists were participating in acts of creation, or perhaps of begetting, in the earth's womb" (Rappaport, 1999, pp. 147, 385). These views lend support to the petitionary-midwife model. The act of engraving or painting each individual animal or plant image was a way of assisting the earth to bring forth by artist midwives who animistically and anthropomorphically perceived the cave as being the origin of life.

In summary, the essence of the intention for Upper Paleolithic cave art is that the animal and few plant images were engraved and painted as petitions to the earth. The almost complete absence of humans lends support to the petitionary-midwife model. There are few human images because the artists were not petitioning for them.

As a result of the innate subconscious perceptual processes of animism, anthropomorphism, dreams, and through the conscious rudimentary reasoning of analogy, the earth was perceived and then gynocentrically conceived to be the female origin that brought forth life from the interior of her body. The cave gave access to the greater interior of the earth, while the narrow areas coated with ochre symbolized menstrual blood and the coming into existence of life. The engravings and paintings of animals and some plants were made by artist midwives as both petitions and assistance to the earth to bring the images into existence. The phenomenon of cave art is more accurately interpreted as the expression of a religious intention and practice.

Cave Artists

Were the Paleolithic cave artists male, female, or did both genders contribute to engraving and painting the animal and plant images? Based upon the prevalence of the physical evidence of hand prints, footprints, and colored dots associated with cave art, it is possible to dispute the view that the depictions were made exclusively by males. In my view, the cave images were petitions by artist midwives to the animistically and anthropomorphically perceived and analogically conceived earth.

There appears to be ample evidence that French male researchers who first reported the finds of Paleolithic cave art androcentrically assumed that it was made by males for a masculine purpose such as hunting or fertility (Nelson, 1997, p. 83; Conkey, 1997, p.174-177). The early view that the art was made exclusively by males for male activities continues to this day. According to most of the theories for cave art, the caves were used by adult males as sites of initiation of young males into the hunt; adult males also produced cave art as decoration, as information about the hunt, to promote fertility and an increase of animals to be hunted; and the art represented myths developed from the visionary experience of male shamans.

I find agreement with Trompf, (1990) who thinks pre-historians have a duty to rewrite prehistory with a recognition of the capacity and contribution of women to the task of producing a living, to reproduction, and to social nurturing during the Paleolithic era. He thinks it is fair to conjecture that just as the presence of both male and female have been found in various degrees in all other known historic religions that both the physical vitality of the male and the female roles of reproduction and nurturing also contributed to Paleolithic religious life (p. 128).

Only two of all of the published depictions of the Paleolithic artists at work represent women, and both were printed in youth and children's literature (Conkey, 1997). Whether women participated in the making of the cave art, one can "assume that survival activities more likely than not absorbed their whole working day."

In other words, women did not have time to be artistic as they were busy taking care of household tasks such as child rearing, food gathering and preparation. It is also argued that the difficult to access location and position of the depictions, such as very high or low areas of the cave would have necessitated physical strength beyond that of a woman (Velo, 1988, p. 309).

These are weak arguments by Velo, as it is difficult to ignore the overwhelming evidence of a gynocentric orientation and female presence in Paleolithic cave art. A few male researchers are willing at least to consider the possibility that women did contribute to the development of Paleolithic art. The view that the Paleolithic art images of vulvas, animals, and female figures are the result of a male "macho" concern with hunting or sexuality is based mostly "on subjective and wishful thinking and ignores the strong possibility that some if not all the artists were female" (Abrahamian, Adams, Bahn & Black, 1987, p. 73).

Clottes & Courtin (1996) venture the hypothesis that in the art of Cosquer cave discovered in 1985, and in my view this could include all of cave art, those animal images having marks interpreted to be projectile weapons or arrows were made by males, while those depictions without any weapon marks were made by female artists. However, they conclude that "It is doubtful that conclusions can ever be reached in this area, but the question is worth raising as a matter for discussion" (p. 177).

Snow (2013) measured handprints from two caves in France including five from Pech Merle, six from Gargas, and 16 handprints from El Castillo in Spain, for a total of 32 handprints. Using a two-step method, he first measured the complete size of the hand utilizing five differing measures to determine adult males from females. The second step measured the ratio of the index finger with the ring finger and the index finger with the pinky fingers to determine adolescent males from females. His results based on the first step showed that only 10 percent of the handprints were those of adult males. The second step results showed 15 percent of the prints were those of adolescent males.

Snow concludes that 75 percent of the cave handprints were those of females. Snow's findings contribute to rebutting earlier androcentric views that the handprints were left by male artists, and to extrapolate a step further, in my view the gender majority who left the handprints also engraved and painted the cave art images.

Some indirect research that bolsters Snow's findings and my own view of the cave artists includes recent genetic research. Through analyzing demographic DNA, hard evidence shows that through all of human history, both prior to the out-of Africa migration and all other later migrations, females have always outnumbered males in any population (Sebastion, L., Xu, H., Ko, A., Li, M. Renaud, G., Butthof, A. Schroder, R. Stoneking, M. (2014)). Therefore, based on population evidence alone, it is probable that more females than males entered the caves, and in so doing as artists left a greater number of stenciled and painted handprints.

The prevalence of small hand prints suggests that the artists were primarily women who were accompanied by their young children, and occasionally, as suggested by a few larger size prints, gynocenrically oriented males. Discovered in 1994 in France, Chauvet cave contains some of the oldest known cave art that has been carbon-dated to 32,000 BP.

Here among the 447 engravings and paintings of 14 species of animals, (Harrington, 1999) researchers found two sequences of hand prints that, judging by known Paleolithic human dimensions and the size and location were made by either an adolescent or a short woman and another set that were the work of a taller individual, possibly a male (Begley, 1999). This evidence suggests that on occasion males did contribute to the making of the art.

Hand prints found in Paleolithic art are either positive, made by coating the palm and fingers and pressing the hand to the rock surface, or they are negative, made by placing the hand on the surface and brushing or blowing paint around it (Seiveking, 1979, p. 46).

A few hand prints have been found engraved on the walls of caves and shelters (Zervos, 1959, p. 81). The hand prints date from the oldest period of the art, circa 31,000-22,000 BP (Clottes & Lewis-Williams, 1998, p. 45).

Hand images are found in 22 caves in France and Spain (Clottes & Courtin, 1996, p. 66). Most often they are negative images. Red and black are the most frequently used colors, while a few are found in yellow and white. Hand prints are found on walls or in niches, isolated, with many grouped together, and some close to animals or dots. After study of the caves of Gargas and El Castillo, researchers found that left hand prints were more frequent than right hand prints. Of this sample, 159 were left hands and 23 were right hands (Ucko & Rosenfeld, 1967, p. 99). It was previously thought that out of all known hand prints 9 out of 10 were of the left hand, but after careful study Leroi-Gourhan (1967) found that right hands were often "placed with the back of the hand against the rock, which explains why certain ones occur in concavities of the wall where the palm-down would not be practical" (p. 148).

Breuil (1979) first referred to a hand print at the French cave of Gargas drawn in black as having four of the fingers cut off (p. 246). Breuil's statements that the hand prints showed evidence of mutilation influenced later researchers (Giedon, 1962, pp. 99-100). Hadingham (1979) reports that among the more than 200 hand prints at Gargas cave, about 50 percent of them have missing fingers (p. 146).

However, after exhaustive on-site research over a period of several years, the view that the hands were mutilated has been found to be erroneous (Clottes & Courtin, 1996, p. 79).

"At Gargas, a considerable number of hands seem to have had fingers cut off or deformed. This has been explained as the result of 'ritual' mutilations. But here again, closer scrutiny suggests that the person who put his hand against the wall bent one or several fingers; the reason for this is not clear, but it did not have mutilation as its cause. In certain cases we can even see that the fingers, originally long, were later retouched to shorten them" (Leroi-Gourhan, 1967, p. 148).

There are few theories for the intention or meaning of the hand prints. Analogically compared with South African Bushman, Leroi-Gourhan (1982) argues that the hand prints were depictions of gestures used by hunters to silently communicate while hunting game animals (p. 58). Another view for the intention of the hand prints, at least those found near animals, is that they were the expression of hunting magic and the hunters taking possession of them (Graziosi, 1960, p. 33). Clottes & Courtin, (1996) doubt that the meaning the hands prints had for the artists will ever be deciphered, (p. 79) and speculate that the hand prints express a "taking possession" of the cave area and so are an "affirmation of power" (p. 173). It is possible, at least in one instance, there may be no intention for the hand prints, as they could be the result of accidently placing the hands on the surfaces during painting of the images (Laming, 1959, p. 96). In a similar manner, the hands could just have been made playfully. The hand prints have also been thought to be a gesture of reverence or perhaps participation in a story or seasonal myth (Marshack, 1991, p. 325). The hand print can also express the personality and presence of the individual, simply meaning, "I was here" (Clottes & Courtin, 1998, p. 136).

Zervos (1959) mentions: "Perhaps one could also see in these hand prints an effective means of putting in action the constraining power of gesture, that of prayer, the hand stretched towards divinity, palm to the outside and open fingers.... One might be tempted to believe that the prayer thus fixed by paint and engraving was intended to be known by the divinity, otherwise one could not explain the discovery of hand prints on the walls of little niches more or less hidden from the view of the crowd" (p. 81) (My translation from the French text)

Of these views, only Marshack's, Clottes & Courtin's, and Zervos' are somewhat relevant. While the hand functions to grasp and to hold, it would serve primarily as an organ of touch. While the entire body, and especially the eyes, were used in the engraving and painting of the animal and plant images, it was the hand that performed the work.

While it was the feet that transported the body into the cave, and the eyes that searched for and found the inchoate partial resemblances of animals and plants in the cave surfaces, it was the hand that enhanced the likeness and so participated in bringing forth the image. So it was the hand image that was left as a record of communion in the assisting of the bringing forth of life from the earth. The significance of the hand prints is that they served as an individual record of contact and as a mark of communion with and participation in bringing forth animal and plant life from the earth, revered by the artists as the female origin of life.

It has been speculated by several researchers that based on the prevalence of small hand prints and footprints found in the caves, the artists and those visiting the cave art areas were primarily women and young children. However, in regard to this view caution has been urged: "It has been claimed on the basis of the size of painted hand impressions that the artists concerned were women or children. Even if it were true that the majority of representations of hands were very small the overlap between the dimensions of male and female hands is so great that sexing on this basis is bound to be dangerous" (Ucko & Rosenfeld, 1967, p. 106).

While this is a relevant point, Ucko & Rosenfeld may be overly cautious. Years of field research and familiarity with the physical dimensions of Paleolithic Homo sapiens sapiens has resulted in the determination that most of the hand prints found in the art caves are too small to have been those of adult males (Leroi-Gourhan, 1967, p. 477).

Snow (2013) also counters Ucko & Rosenfeld's claim with his findings of hand prints from the Paleolithic caves compared with his findings from modern humans. His conclusion is that there was greater "sexual dimorphism" or genetic hand size differences during the Paleolithic between male and female hand size than in modern populations. Yet admittedly, there will always remain some hand prints for which it will not be possible to ascertain gender with size measurements as the only criteria.

Bahn (1997) also is skeptical of the possibility that the artists were women or children and remarks that, "Some scholars have recently begun to wonder whether a good deal of cave art might not have been produced by children or adolescents" but aside from finger-markings, smaller hand prints and crudely drawn images, he dismisses the possibility, arguing that only an experienced adult artist could have produced the vast majority of sophisticated art images (p. 36).

I would substitute the words females or women for Bahn's use of the word "adolescents" in his statement; then the excursion into the caves would make more sense. The smaller so-called adolescent hand prints and footprints were most likely those of young mothers bringing their children along. Rice (1982) observes that based on the evidence of historic hunting and gathering groups, females during the Paleolithic era had their first menstruation between 10 and 12 years old, and gave birth on average every three years (pp. 406-407). This suggests that the footprints of so-called adolescents found in the caves were also those of young mothers accompanied by their children.

In referring to the artists who left their hand prints at Gargas, Barriere (1976) asks, "Were the men of Gargas painting their hands or making negatives on the cave walls?" (p. 83). In his long-term study of the hand prints at Gargas, Barriere first spoke of the artist's hand prints as having been made exclusively by males (pp. 42, 47). While Barriere does mention the presence of a "baby's hand," (p. 56) he does not expressly mention anywhere in his in-depth study the possibility that some of the hand prints could have been made by women.

However, in a brief article appearing eight years later, Barriere (1984) corrects this omission by commenting that the hand prints were not only those of males and babies, but also included children and women (p. 518). Barriere's previous view of the presence of adult male hand prints at Gargas is also contradicted by one of the former leading authorities in the field of European Paleolithic art.

"In most cases the hands are too small to have belonged to men: the majority seem to be women's hands, and some obviously belonged to children...All the hands at Gargas are those of children, or at any rate are smaller than those of an adult male" (Leroi-Gourhan, 1967, p. 477). These assertions by Leroi-Gourhan, an acknowledged research authority in Paleolithic art, support the view that the majority of hand prints found in Paleolithic art are those of women and children and that all of the hand prints at Gargas are those of women and children.

It has been confirmed by other researchers that among the hand prints at Gargas cave, there are several that belong to babies only a few months old (Hadingham, 1979, p. 146). The hand print of a young child at Gargas shows the arm was being held by an adult while it was made (Clottes & Lewis-Williams, 1998, p. 98). It has been posited that children were not afraid to explore the depths of the caves either alone or accompanied by adults (Bahn & Vertut, 1997, p. 10).

I was fortunate to visit the caves of Gargas and Bedeilhac located in the French Pyrenees, and the grotto of Pech Merle in central France during March 2001. I did not have a special government permit required to enter the more difficult to access and non-public areas of the cave. However, based upon my observation I was able at least partially to visually confirm Leroi-Gourhan's and other researchers' observations pertaining to a number of the negative hand prints at Gargas. The size of the palms and length and width of the fingers of the larger prints appeared to be narrow, indicating either female hands or possibly those of an adolescent male. In one area of the cave, located perhaps two feet from the floor, were several negative child's hand prints in red ochre.

At the cave of Bedeilhac where the art has been dated to circa 15,000 BP, I observed young adult and children's hand prints still apparent in the clay floor at several locations around sculpted animal figures nearly 800 meters into the cave. However, at Pech Merle, at least some of the negative hand prints in blue-black manganese displayed larger palms and shorter and thicker finger size. Six of these prints were referred to by the guide as "mains d' home" or the hands of a male.

While these larger size hand prints could have been those of a female, the hand size also suggests that at least on occasion, males did participate in the making of the animal and plant cave images. The additional evidence of smaller footprints accompanied by very young children contributes support to the view that the vast majority of smaller hand prints left by the artists were those of women.

Approximately 1,000 footprints were left by Upper Paleolithic artists and by those who accompanied them into the caves (Pfeiffer, 1983, p. 43). Footprints found in the mud of some of the art caves, for example, Niaux, Aldene, and Pech Merle, suggest that many of those visiting the deeper parts of the caves were children 10-13 years of age (Ucko & Rosenfeld, 1967, p. 106). In the Upper Paleolithic caves, it is striking that "practically all known footprints were made by young people" (Leroi-Gourhan, 1967, p. 181). Most of the footprints found in French caves during the Ice Age and later are those of children, suggesting a lack of fear of the cave environment (Bahn, 1997, p. 36). In my view, the evidence specifically suggests a lack of fear by young women and their children.

At Pech Merle cave I personally observed 10 partial footprints and two that were distinct, preserved in the once-mud floor, now covered with a clear coating of calcite deposit. These were referred to by the cave guide and by the onsite museum display as the footprints of an adolescent male. However, based on my observation of the rather narrow shape, I would argue that the footprints could have just as well have been those of a young female.

"Whenever Paleolithic footprints have been found in deep caves, they include…children's footprints. Several authors...have argued that this was for initiation ceremonies. This idea is contradicted by the fact that some of these children were far too young. The footprints of a three-year old are preserved in Le Tuc d' Audoubert and the hand prints of a five or six-year old in Fontanet" (Clottes, 1997, p. 211). In my view, the footprints and hand prints of "adolescents," accompanied by the footprints and hand prints of very young children in the deep caves, are convincing evidence of female artists accompanied by their young children.

Many of the hand prints are found proximal to what have been referred to as "dots" (Bahn & Vertut, 1997, p. 195). The painted dots found in the caves are usually red or black and vary in size from just a few millimeters to more than 10 centimeters. The colored dots date from the beginning of Paleolithic art circa 32,000 BP until near the end circa 10,000 BP. Many colored dots have recently been found in the art of Chauvet cave dated to circa 32,000 BP, (Chauvet, Deschamps & Hillaire, 1996) and dots are present in the cave art of Marsoulas dated to circa 10,000 BP (Giedion, 1962, pp. 147, 149). Dots aligned in rows or grouped frequently mark the beginning point of art images in the deep parts of the cave, as well as the furthest end in a terminal cul de sac (Leroi-Gourhan, 1982, p. 56). They are also found on, above, or below animal images.

Chauvet et al. (1996) point out that at Chauvet cave in southeast France, "The most frequent and characteristic signs are the groups of circular dots." Here the mostly red dots measuring six to eight centimeters in diameter mark the edge of panels, and are often arranged in vertical lines, rectangular, and semi-circular shapes. Two large panels consist of 100 dots or more, and another large group of dots suggests the shape of a bison or mammoth (pp. 25-28, 103). At the grotto of Pech Merle I observed numerous black dots that fill the bodies of the two horses, and there are numerous black dots that are interspersed with approximately one dozen red dots that surround the figures.

There are few speculations as to the intention for the dots in cave art. They may have "represented different concepts according to their number and disposition" (Leroi-Gourhan, 1982, p. 56). The dots, spots, and pock marks all had one meaning, and that is "life-force...dots mean animal life or reproduction or are used to generate it" (Smith, 1992, p. 117). Giedion 1962) argues that the dots represent a "desire for procreation" of the animals, (p. 151) but he offers no explanation for his view. After recent research of the cave art at Lascaux, Rappenglueck speculates that he has discovered the oldest lunar calendar.

He points out that 13 dots near a shape somewhat resembling a square represents one-half of the moon cycle while the geometric form symbolizes the moon. He also thinks that another group of 27 dots represent each day of the lunar cycle (News in Science, 2000).

Leroi-Gourhan's explanation for the dots is vague, while Rappenglueck's is a highly speculative and isolated example. If the 13 dots represent half of a moon cycle, this would be 26 days, which is close to the 27 dots said to be the number of days of the complete lunar cycle. While not accurate this is close to the length of the moon cycle, today observed to be 29.5 days. However, the view that a square shape represents the moon is a stretch of the imagination.

I find more agreement with Smith's view that the dots represented a single meaning; and that they were associated with or used to generate animal life is an important speculation. The colored dots often mark the beginning and end of the sections of the cave where the images are located. Having observed this characteristic while visiting the cave of Bedeilhac, I think that the dots were placed there by the artists to denote to visitors areas of the cave especially chosen by the artists in which to petition and to assist the earth to bring forth or send the painted and engraved animal and plant images. The red and black dots often found in association with the female hand prints were left as a record of the religious activity of petitioning and assisting the earth to bring the animal images to life.

The red dots have also been found associated with other parts of female anatomy. In the Le Combel gallery of Pech Merle, in a passage located just prior to entering the inmost cave chamber, is a stalactite shape resembling a female breast surrounded by 20 red dots (Giedion, 1962, pp. 214-215).

In my view, the red and black painted dots are symbolic of female blood shed during menstruation. When found on or around animal depictions, the dots represent menstrual drops of blood placed there primarily by women or gynocentrically oriented male artists to assist the images to be born from the earth and so be hunted and killed for food.

In support of the view, that the dots represent the menstrual blood of life, there is a report of a find in the Ignateva cave near Yamazy-Tash located in the southern Ural mountains of Russia, and dating to the late Upper Paleolithic or Mesolithic era circa 8,000 BP, of a "female figure with 28 red dots between her legs, a depiction which seems clearly to refer to the menstrual cycle" (Rudgley, 1999, p. 196). In this instance, the evidence convincingly suggests that the dots were symbolic of menstrual blood.

Speculatively, females could have entered the cave during their menstrual cycles, commingling their own blood with red ochre to make the red dots on the cave wall, and left hand prints to confirm their visit. It would be interesting to test the red dot areas for any residue of human blood. However, the dots were surely symbolic of drops of menstrual blood, the "red for fresh blood and the black for dried blood." Eventually in Levantine art during the Mesolithic and Neolithic eras, circa 10,000-6,000 BP, the dots continue to symbolize blood, but during this time the dots represent the life blood of hunted and wounded animals. Beltran (1982) observes that as used in later Levantine art, lines of red dots "represent the trail of blood from wounded animals" (p. 37).

Summary

I have investigated the phenomena of Paleolithic hand prints, footprints, and the red and black colored dots associated with cave art, and the theories offered by researchers to explain these artifacts. Through not indulging in specious analogical reasoning I thereby reached the following conclusions.

The essential meaning of these three phenomena is that the hand prints were made as a record of contact and as a gesture of communion and participation in the bringing forth of animal and occasionally plant life from the earth, animistically and anthropomorphically perceived to be the female origin of life.

Based on the prevalence of smaller size hand prints and footprints, the evidence suggests that the artists were primarily women accompanied by their children and on occasion gynocentrically oriented males. The red and black dots often found in conjunction with the hand prints and animal images are symbolic drops of blood shed during menstruation and are therefore primarily associated with women and the coming into existence of life.

These phenomena of cave art contribute further support to the petitionary-midwife model that the Paleolithic artists were primarily women who acted as midwives in assisting the earth to bring forth life. The engravings and paintings of animals were made by artist midwives as both "petitions and assistance" to the earth to bring forth the images into existence, and is therefore the expression of a geocentric and gynocentric religious intention and practice.

Further evidence of an anomaly involving the discrepancy between the fauna found at Paleolithic living sites and the animal images of the art caves provides additional support for the petitionary-midwife theory.

Animal Image and Faunal Anomaly

A phenomenon has been observed at many rock-shelter and cave living sites that provides credible support for the petitionary-midwife model. The species of animals depicted in the cave art contrasts with the discovered remains of the animals eaten by the inhabitants. Since this is such a striking point, and at first glance appears to contradict the petitionary-midwife model. This discrepancy demands further investigation (Hadingham, 1979, pp. 207-208).

The evidence from many sites is that the depicted species of animals do not correspond to the quantity and remains of species consumed. At Lascaux, reindeer remains comprise 90 per cent of the bones but their image was drawn only once. Horses make up 60 per cent of the images, but are not found in the bones. Images of bison, auroch, and ibex are found in the cave art, but there are no bone remains. For boar and roe deer this situation is reversed (Bahn & Vertut, 1997, p. 177).

" the ibex dominates the art of Pair-non-Pair but is absent from its fauna; at Comarque over 75 per cent of the bones are reindeer, but the figures are mainly horses, at Villars the people ate reindeer but did not draw any; in many Ardeche caves, the mammoth predominates in the art (almost half of the figures), and the ibex and reindeer are absent, whereas the bones show an abundance of the last two species and an absence of mammoth; at Gargas, there are no reindeer figures although over a third of the bones are of that species, but the mammoth, absent from the fauna, was depicted six times...at Altimira they drew bison and ate red deer; at Elkain the thirty-four horses are 57.6 percent of the animal figures, but there are almost no horse bones in the fauna which is dominated by ibex and red deer" (p. 177-179).

There are few equivalents between animals depicted and faunal remains in any sample of the excavated remains. The choices for the cave images differ from the food choices as found in the remains (Bahn & Vertut, 1997, p. 179).

In southwest France the reindeer provided 90-98 % of the diet, yet it was the horse and bison that were portrayed most. Hadingham (1979) asks, "What inhibition can have deterred the artists from portraying their most important food animal" (pp. 207-208)? Reindeer were the most hunted and eaten animal during the Upper Paleolithic era. In the archeological remains of bones at Lascaux, those of the reindeer comprised the majority, 88.7 percent.

However only one image of a reindeer is found on the cave walls (Ruspoli, 1986, pp. 49, 57). "Why were the animals most frequently represented by the artists, such as the bison, the aurochs and the ibex, not eaten? And why does the horse, which is by far the most frequently depicted animal in the paintings and engravings, account for only 0.8 per cent of the food remains, and the red deer for only 1.5 per cent, compared with the reindeer 88.7 per cent" (p. 49)?

This statistic raises questions about the meaning of Paleolithic art and flagrantly contradicts the hunting magic theory. According to this theory, the most hunted animal should be the one most depicted, so there should be many images of reindeer at Lascaux (p. 49).

“The remains of wild boar and roe deer are plentiful in prehistoric encampment sites...the almost complete absence of these two animals in the prehistoric cave pictures is somewhat surprising. They were among the game animals eaten but, for reasons unknown to us, not depicted” (pp. 57-58).

From bone remains it is evident that Upper Paleolithic humans did consume birds, yet it is difficult to satisfactorily explain their rarity in cave art. One explanation is that birds are not easy prey, and secondly, they are not as worthy prey as are the larger animals (Ucko & Rosenfeld, 1967, p. 183). Yet these views are hardly convincing. Since avian remains are very common in the fauna, the birds were easy to capture and were evidently worthy prey. Birds and fish, common sources of food at the time (as shown by their bones in the inhabited areas) are rarely drawn; wolf and fox, commonly found in the cave rubbish, are also very rarely drawn...bird’s bones are so common in the kitchen refuse of the period, showing that they must have been an important part of Upper Paleolithic man’s diet, [yet] they were so seldom drawn on the walls of the caves (Sieveking & Sieveking, 1966, pp. 27, 33). Most of the bird species portrayed in Paleolithic art are waterfowl, while the remains show that these are the least common of the birds consumed (Sieveking, 1979, p. 149).While many researchers point out the discrepancy between animals depicted and faunal remains, few offer an explanation for this anomaly.

One explanation for the variation of the animal images depicted is that, over the long course of thousands of years differing concepts and myths developed and caused a change in the choices of animals portrayed (Bahn, 1998, p. 139). This seems to be a rationalist explanation, that is, using conscious reasoning early humans conceived various myths or stories over time and chose various animals to represent these tales.

Another explanation for the discrepancy between animals depicted and the availability and faunal remains is that the artists just liked to think about them rather than consume them (Conkey, 1981, p. 23).

While this view is very close to the theory of art for art's sake, it could be credible, especially as regards the art found in rock-shelters and near the entrance of caves. However, since at least half of the art is located in the depths of caves and is heavily super-impositioned, this view is not convincing.

Mithen (1988) points out that while the reindeer and red deer were portrayed the least frequently in Upper Paleolithic cave art, the faunal remains of these two animals were the most numerous. His explanation for the fauna consisting mostly of red deer and reindeer is that these remains are the result of large cooperative hunts. These successful group hunts resulted in less-available animals and so the predictive ability of the hunters declined. During times of lower animal population and thus low success of group hunting, hunters turned to stalking individual animals. Artists depicted individual animals as an "information flow." Portraying the animals was a way to prepare mentally for the hunt by facilitating visual recall of the animal and its associated tracks and behaviors, so as to increase hunting success of small groups or individual hunters.

Mithen combines a variation of the long advocated hunting theory with the more recent art as information theory. However, again, at least half of the art is located in the depths of caves and is often heavily super-impositioned. What practical purpose concerning information was served by traveling so far into the cave depths? Since many of the cave images are super-impositioned or overlaid with multiple depictions, it is not convincing this would have contributed to accurate visual recall of information about the animal.

Rice & Paterson (1985) surveyed the data of animals portrayed in the cave art, and found it to consist mainly of reindeer, bovines, horse, ibex, red deer, and mammoth. These total 93 percent of the 1,955 depictions from 90 cave sites located in southwest France. The bone data was collected from reports of 408 excavated layers of 151 living sites that span the entire Upper Paleolithic era circa 35,000-10,000 BP. While reindeer images were 9.8 percent of the total depictions, the bone remains were 28.8 percent.

Red deer are also under-portrayed being 6.9 percent of the images and 15.4 percent of bone remains. Most common of the animals portrayed were bovines that made up 37 percent of the total images while their bone remains were 22.4 percent; and horse images were 33.4 percent of the total while their bone remains were 26.4 percent.

Rice & Paterson first suggest that the animals portrayed were either the result of food and meat yield preference, or the animals most feared as a result of the danger in hunting them. They surveyed game and hunting specialists to determine the most dangerous species. These were determined to be the mammoth, bovines, and horse; and these are over-portrayed while the under-portrayed reindeer and deer are less dangerous. The intention for the art is then ambiguously stated to be related to either fertility or hunting, including hunting magic, education, or story-telling. Rice & Paterson note that during the end of the Paleolithic era known as the Azilian era circa 10,000 BP, the faunal remains indicate small game hunting and collecting and the art no longer portrays the larger animal images. While Rice and Paterson do not comment on this phenomenon, utilizing their theory one could presume this suggests these smaller creatures were then no longer preferred or feared as a result of their size.

In a follow-up article Rice & Paterson (1986) finally conclude that the primary stimulus for the Paleolithic art of both France and Spain was the economic contribution of meat yield. However, among the animals listed in the study as being rarely portrayed in cave art are elk, fallow deer, saiga antelope, musk-ox, and wild donkey. According to Rice & Paterson's final view that the animals were represented according to the amount of meat yield, then the rarely depicted large elk, fallow deer, saiga antelope, and musk-oxen, as well as the never depicted wild boar, the remains of which are so plentiful in prehistoric camp sites, (Ruspoli, 1986, pp 57-58) should have been much more prevalent in the cave art images as well.

Therefore Rice & Paterson's view is not convincing to explain the discrepancy between the depicted images and the faunal remains of those animals eaten.

Discussion

As a phenomenon of Paleolithic art, the animal image-faunal anomaly is important and worthy of attention and discussion. Of the theories that seek to explain the animal image-faunal anomaly, only Laming (1959) comes close to the artists' meaning or intention for the animal images. She thinks there were a number of factors for the choice of animals images, including, "psychological, magical, or religious which cannot be explained so long as the purpose of the underground sanctuaries is unknown" (p. 126). Laming mentions these factors but she does not elaborate on them.

After researching the Paleolithic anomaly consisting of a discrepancy between the animals depicted in contrast to the faunal remains, and the theories that seek to explain the phenomenon, I would agree with Laming, that the essential meaning for the phenomenon of frequently portraying certain animals, the fauna of which are minimally present in the remains, consists of psychological, religious, and physiological but not magical factors. Psychologically, since early humans lived completely dependent on the natural environment, it is safe to speculate that they noticed the plants growing from the interior of the earth and the young of animals and insects being born and coming from dens.

Based on observation, they perceived the earth animistically to be a living form; the artists found shapes in the cave surface that resembled an animal and then enhanced the feature into a finished depiction. Second, the earth was perceived anthropomorphically to be a female origin and the religious factor is evident in the placing of the animal images on the cave surfaces as petitions and assistance to the earth to bring forth life. The depictions of the animals are expressions of petitionary desires by artist midwives who were assisting the earth to give birth to the living forms so they could be hunted and harvested. Third, the cave images represent not magical but physical desires to consume certain animals that were not immediately present.

The contradiction between animal images portrayed and the confirmed remains of those eaten suggests the meaning Upper Paleolithic art had for the artists. This phenomenon supports the petitionary-midwife theory that the artists were asking for what they did not have enough of, the animals portrayed.

A few of the art caves depict predatory or dangerous animals such as rhinos, lions, cave bears, and mammoths. An example of this can be found in Chauvet cave discovered in 1994 in the south of France. Jean Clottes, leader and member of the research team that explored the cave, explains that in the portraying of these animals the artists were seeking "to capture the essence" of these particular species that for them "symbolized danger, strength, and power" (Begley, 1999). His remarks suggest that since these animals were dangerous, the depictions had nothing to do with the hunting or consumption of them.

My view is that the artists were not interested in capturing the symbolic "essence" of the animals, but were primarily interested in actually physically capturing and killing the animals for food. Even though the healthy adult lion and bear were dangerous, and the adult rhino and mammoth were large and powerful, and therefore potentially dangerous, the infirm and young of these species would have been more easily hunted and killed for food.

The engravings and paintings of all the animal species are petitions drawn primarily by women midwives, and on occasion gynocentrically oriented males, to assist the earth to give birth to or send the desired animal to be hunted and killed and thereby provide food.

Conclusion

Concluding discussion of the petitionary-midwife hypothesis, I present the following findings. I have investigated the artifacts of Paleolithic cave art and the theories offered to explain this phenomenon.

I then proceeded to reduce analogical association and comparison with what is known of these artifacts and conclude that Upper Paleolithic cave art is an interaction with the earth in a meaningful way. The cognitive basis for this behavioral interaction by Paleolithic humans was that the earth was animistically perceived to be a living entity, and that the interior of the earth was specifically perceived anthropomorphically and conceived analogically to be a female form. Evidence to support this view includes speculation that since Paleolithic humans were foragers they observed the cyclical growth of plants from within the earth, and the young of animals and insects coming from dens. These observations contributed to the animistic perception that the interior of the earth was the origin of life. The enhancing of natural shapes occurring in the cave surfaces that resembled an animal also suggests the innate perceptual process of animism.

The use of red ochre to paint animal images, to coat narrow and oval-shaped areas of the cave, and the pieces of bone and teeth that were placed in the cleft areas of the wall situated near ochre smudges and reliefs, all suggest the perceptual process of anthropomorphism. Since the color red appears infrequently in the environment, this suggests that the primary use of ochre was associated with menstrual blood and life.

Paleolithic humans could not comprehend the cave to be a geologic formation. Seeking comprehension of the mysterious presence of the cave, they perceived it anthropomorphically to be the female origin of animal and plant life. Anthropomorphizing the interior of the cave to be a female-like womb that brought forth life, suggests an overall gynocentric orientation.

The ability for rudimentary reasoning as suggested by imitation in tool-making, of making one tool like another, also contributed to analogically conceiving the cave interior to be similar to the place within the female body that brought forth life.

Having similar brain structure, Paleolithic peoples dreamed as do modern humans. The innate subconscious perceptual process of the vivid imagery of dreams experienced in sleep and recalled during waking consciousness also served to inspire the artists to make the depictions.

Sustaining life completely dependent on the natural environment contributed to the development of a geocentric orientation. The animal images were petitions geocentrically directed to the interior of the earth as the origin of animal and plant life. The cave artists were primarily women who by drawing the images based on the memory of sensory observation and perceived dream images acted as midwives in petitioning and assisting the earth to give birth. Based on the prevalence of smaller hand prints and footprints, the evidence suggests that the artists were primarily women accompanied by children, and on occasion, gynocentrically oriented males. The red and black dots often found in conjunction with the hand prints and animal images are symbolic of fresh and dried drops of blood shed during menstruation and are associated with women and the coming into existence of life.

The phenomenon of the animal image-faunal anomaly, the discrepancy between the animals depicted in the cave art and the confirmed faunal remains, also provides convincing support for the petitionary midwife theory. The artists were asking for and assisting the earth, perceived to be the greater female origin of life, to provide what they did not have, the animals depicted. Like burial, cave art is an expression of an earth cultus, a geocentric and gynocentric religion.

Chapter 5

Male Figures

The topic of male figures in Paleolithic cave art is important enough to merit a separate investigation and discussion. In what follows I will examine what have been interpreted to be male figures in cave art during the Upper Paleolithic era circa 35,000-13,000 BP. The engraved and painted figures claimed to be male, mainly by male researchers, have either been inadvertently misinterpreted, or androcentrically and anthropocentrically intentionally manipulated so as to promote the point of view that male images are present in Paleolithic art and that therefore males were the primary makers of the depictions. These debatable cave images can be better explained as the result of super-impositioning, as anthropomorphized animals, and as products of creative imagination by the artists.

This investigation is related to the petitionary-midwife model, as the convincing lack of male images in cave art prior to 13,000 BP contributes additional support to the theory, that there was prevalent during that time a general gynocentric orientation and that the cave artists were primarily females who on occasion might have been assisted by gynocentrically oriented males.

I have researched and examined the Paleolithic cave images prior to circa 13,000 BP that have been most reputed to be evidence of a male depiction, and briefly some of the lesser known depictions. I also investigated the various views concerning the assertion that human males are present in the images of Paleolithic art during this time. What follows is both a discussion and a critique of the views for and against the presence of human males in the cave images of Paleolithic art, and my findings.

Most of the theories that seek to explain Upper Paleolithic cave art assume that it was exclusively made by males, and that male images present in a very few depictions support this assertion. This is a biased androcentric point of view for which there is little evidence.

Henri Breuil (1877-1961) the French pre-historian and artist was the most influential individual in reproducing and interpreting many of the cave art images. Beginning in 1900, Breuil recorded hundreds of Paleolithic cave images by using thin sheets of paper held over the artwork and tracing them with crayon or pencil. Over the years his authoritative sketching has been reproduced in many publications and has greatly influenced the perception and interpretation of Paleolithic art. However, more recent examination of his renderings has revealed at least some subjective and even inaccurate representations. Many times Breuil either misidentified or misinterpreted animal images. He identified an animal image as a boar, which more recently has been accurately identified as a bison (Halverson, 1992, p. 399). In other renditions, some of his works have also been shown to be inaccurate (Bahn & Vertut, 1997, pp. 49-51).

Through the years, there has been a tendency to identify certain images as human, and especially as male. Supposed human depictions have been identified as such without prior consideration of criteria for doing so. Interpretations have often been biased by anthropomorphism, hunting-magic theories, or ethnic comparisons (Clottes, 1989, p. 34). Breuil's work shows evidence of having been influenced by each of these influences. His rendering of the image popularly known as the "sorcerer or shaman of Les Trois Freres, France is an example. Being a Catholic abbe or priest, it is perhaps reasonable that Breuil (1979) should be influenced to say that the figure is the theistic "God" of Les Trois Freres (pp. 170, 176) thereby characterizing the figure as an anthropomorphic male deity. However, rethinking his view, he finally concluded that the figure was more likely, "the Spirit controlling the multiplication of game and hunting expeditions" (p. 176). This view is based on analogy with historic cultures known to have had a "Master of Animals," an anthropomorphized animal who sent or withheld game from the hunters as a way of explaining the causality of a failed or successful hunt. When Breuil's version of the figure is contrasted with a recent drawing of the same image, it is easy to understand the criticism of his proclivity to fill in lines (Bahn & Vertut, 1997, p. 189).

His elaboration is obvious when compared with a more accurate copy of the original (Ucko & Rosenfeld, 1967, p. 206). The acceptance of the view that some of the art images were male dancers clothed in animal skins and wearing masks was based mostly on the sorcerer of Les Trois Freres figure, (Hadingham, 1979) and it was Breuil (1979) who first referred to the image as a sorcerer or magician clad in a ritual costume (p. 182).

The figure known as the sorcerer or shaman of Les Trois Freres, dated to circa 15,000 BP, (Clottes & Lewis-Williams, 1998, p. 54) is located in a vertical shaft four meters above the cave floor and is the only image to be painted in black outline. The image, 75 centimeters high and 37.5 centimeters long, is described as having “cervid ears and horns and a horselike tail, joined to human or semi-human parts such as staring eyes, a pointed beard, and genitals (though these are placed in an odd position)” (The Sorcerer, 1999). Other descriptions include the head is turned to the left; it has the eyes of an owl, the antlers and ears of a stag, the body and legs resemble a human, the genitals are placed where a feline’s should be rather than a human, it has the tail of a horse, and a beak for a nose; (Pfeiffer, 1982, p. 107) it has the “horns of a deer, the paws of a bear, the eyes of an owl, the tail of a wolf or of a horse;” (Blanc, 1966, p. 121) the figure has the eyes of either an owl, a lion, or a ghost, it has the antlers, ears, and the shoulders of a reindeer, the tail of a horse, a human-like sex organ, “but located where a feline’s would be” (Leroi-Gourhan, 1967, p. 132). Based on an overall consensus, the image could be that of a partially, poorly, or imaginatively drawn bear or lion.

Dickson (1990) calls attention to an important characteristic of the figure, portrayed as an “upright...hunched, bipedal creature [that] has reindeer antlers and ears, an owlish face that ends in a human beard, bear paws...a horse’s tail and a large, flaccid human penis” (p. 115). Based on the upright posture, some researchers argue that the image is a symbolic figure representing what a male shaman might have experienced, such as transformation into various animals during an altered state of consciousness (Lommel, 1967, p. 128).

The more upright posture in which it is usually presented suggests an effort to manipulate the image to convince the viewer that this is actually an image of a human male disguised or in a costume of animal parts. Hadingham (1979) observes that rather than standing straight or upright, the image is actually closer to being "on all fours, not the vertical pose in which it is usually reproduced in many books" (p. 183). Upon closer examination, the image does not appear to be either completely upright or on all fours, but certainly closer to being on all fours rather than being upright. Elaboration of the image by Breuil, and the intentional placing of the image by other researchers in more of an upright position as if dancing (Breuil, 1979, p. 176) convincingly suggests a cognitive tendency for anthropomorphism and androcentrism and is therefore not an accurate presentation of the image.

Another well-known image at Les Trois-Freres drawn and identified by Breuil is usually interpreted and accepted to be a male "sorcerer with bow." The engraved figure, dated to circa 15,000 BP, (Clottes & Lewis-Williams, 1998, p. 54) is described as a bison that, "seems to be dancing on one hind leg; the knee appears human but the leg is that of a bison; the very conspicuous sexual parts are those of a bison. The result is a somewhat puzzling figure" (Leroi-Gourhan, 1967, p.132). Here only the knee is said to be human-like. The image is usually presented in isolation, yet it is only a small part of a heavily super-impositioned panel. The interpretation that the figure represents a human is overly subjective. The inclination to identify the figure as a male human also suggests a tendency for an anthropocentric and androcentric bias.

The image certainly is puzzling if assumed to be a male human dressed as an animal. Based on what appears to be a human knee, lower leg, and foot, Breuil (1979) identifies the figure as a human using a "musical bow," (p. 177) while the entire rest of the image, which is distinctly a bison, is ignored. Upon closer examination, by turning the image to the side, it is easy to see that rather than a male human drawn with animal characteristics, the image is mis-traced, so that the lines of the animal's left leg are actually part of the animal immediately above.

Having observed the phenomenon of super-impositioning at the Paleolithic caves of Gargas and Pech Merle, I am convinced that careful study is required to be able accurately to separate and identify the multiple images. Caution has been urged in the copying of parietal or cave art images since, "There are hazards in copying a drawing on a wall. If it is worn or entangled with other drawings its decipherment must, to some degree, be subjective" (Sieveking, 1979, pp. 37-38). This is a reasonable explanation for what has occurred. However, rather than merely being an accidental identification by researchers as a result of the super-impositioned tangle of many other animal images, based on the usual presentation of the image in isolation and in an upright posture, it is reasonable to also suspect an anthropocentric and androcentric bias in the misidentification of the depiction.

Other unusual images found in the Le Trois Freres cave art dating from circa 15,000 BP, include a bear with a wolf's head and a bear with a bison's tail. Maringer (1960) explains these unusual images by arguing that the artists were fearful of portraying the bear "as it really was," or that the images were "intended to portray men disguised as bears" (p. 103). However, my view is that these images might be better attributed to super-impositioning and/or simply a creative imagination.

Perhaps the most discussed scene in all of Paleolithic cave art, is the so-called "Bird Man" at Lascaux dated to circa 18,000 BP (Clottes & Lewis-Williams, 1998, p. 54). Comments by various researchers include: "the head wears a bird mask with a prominent beak. The penis is shown erect, indicating death by severance of the backbone...a bird-headed man...his four fingers open...a black stroke indicating the phallus...camouflaged as an animal (Davenport & Jochim, 1988, p. 558). The figure is reputed to be a shaman "bird/man," and the human footprints found in various other caves are said to belong to the "students of elders and shamans" who conducted rites or rituals there (pp. 560-561).

The interpretation of this image as a male human provides further convincing evidence of the cognitive tendency for anthropocentrism and androcentrism by researchers.

Identification of the image as male in disguise or as the vision of a shaman is based on the supposed hands, legs, feet, and phallus. When considered closely however, the so-called digits of the hands are actually feathers at the end of the wings. In most line and photo reproductions (Irwin, 2000, p. 297) the lower half of the right wing is omitted, perhaps inadvertently but most probably intentionally making the appendage appear to be an arm rather than the actual wing shape. A better image of what appears to be the full wing is apparent in a photograph. The legs appear elongated or exaggerated, while the feet are not those of a human. The so-called bird-man is simply an elongated bird. What is said to be a phallus is the awkwardly placed bird's tail, which is simply not in perspective, extended upward rather than into the background, due to a lack of artistic technique. The view of most researchers, that the figure is an ichthyphallic man with a spear at his side who has just been killed by a disemboweled bison, is a highly doubtful and unlikely interpretation.

A find in 1991 of what is said to be a male human has occurred at Cosquer cave in the south of France, where visits based on charcoal remains left by early humans have been carbon-dated to circa 26,000-19,000 BP (Clottes & Courtin, 1996). While the depiction is confirmed to be "sexually indeterminate," the chapter that discusses the image is entitled, "the killed man," (p. 155) and suggests an androcentric bias. Since there is a lack of gender identity, a more accurate heading for the chapter would certainly be, the "killed human." The image, approximately 25 centimeters in length, was originally identified as a seal. After some study by the researchers, this early impression was deemed a mistake. The image was later identified to be not a "naturalistic human," but rather only the "idea" of a human (p. 156).

"The individual is depicted lying on its back but in a slightly slanted position, with arm and leg extended upward. The head is small, rounded or oval in shape, and the nose can just be made out....The body has a roughly rectangular shape, with a...curve in the back.

A pronounced curve shapes the rump. The lower limb, much shortened, is sketched in a cursory way.... A human figure has been represented on its back, arms and legs extended, as if falling. It was first overlaid by a light mark, before being annihilated by a terrible weapon. It represents a human killed, or rather the *idea* of a human killed, and is not a naturalistic depiction....The three light but clear marks on top of the head that are reminiscent of a seal's mustache, and the lower limb that has been shortened and tapered, may equally well have been intended to make this human more like a pinniped" [a seal] (pp. 155-156).

While the idea that the depiction is a human exists in the minds of the researchers, the evidence is not convincing that this idea was in the mind of the artist. This assertion is based on the following observations. Neither the body shape nor the visible half of the head area is convincingly human. What is said to be the "leg" of the figure is not convincing as it consists of a triangular shape and has no foot. The depiction is said to have "a very elongated arm ending in an obvious hand, with the fingers depicted by several deeply engraved parallel lines" (p. 155). What is identified as an upper arm, intersects with the middle of the figure and consists of a fluted or scraped elongation in the rock surface that appears to have no relationship to the engraved figure. What are said to be fingers is also not convincing as they appear to be gouged and worn areas that are not at all related to the engraving. The "nose" appears formed by a small triangular fragment of rock naturally missing from an intersecting engraved line through the head area of the image.

Since it has the overall body shape, marks resembling a "seal's mustache," and a short tapered lower limb that resembles that of a seal, the depiction is most likely a seal or other composite or imaginary animal that has only two human-like attributes of buttocks and the partial oval-shaped head. The depiction should be more accurately classified, as Clottes & Courtin do (p. 123) with several other images in the cave, as an "indeterminate animal," (pp. 113, 120-123) some of which include either a "composite animal," (p. 122) or a "fantasy animal" (pp. 112).

It is sensible to insist on a minimal description of what is present, and to reduce interpretive reasoning based on association and the use of analogy. However, after the evidence is presented that the depiction represents a human, this view is bolstered by a chained argument and presentation of other reputed "wounded man" images that are hardly convincing. These male images are those located at the caves of Cougnac, Pech Merle and Sous-Grand-Lac, and Gabillou (pp. 157-159). There are also two purported male images at Le Portel (Lorblanchet, 1989, p. 131). However, all of these depictions are even less convincing as male images. To bolster support that these are indeed human male images, they are in turn all analogized or compared with an engraving of a recognizable male pierced with arrows located in a rock-shelter in Spain and dating to the much later Bronze Age circa 5,000 BP (p. 160). When the Cosquer cave depiction is presented alone, the argument that it is the image of a human and that it portrays a "murder" or "execution" scene, (p. 161) is not convincing. The assertion that the depiction is a "killed man," cannot withstand scrutiny on its own merit as evidenced by the use of analogy to provide support for this weak view.

Not only is the interpretation that the depiction is a killed human not convincing but the view that the long forked line and the two shorter lines that intersect the figure are a projectile weapon also is not convincing. The shape formed by the interconnecting lines does not convincingly an "enormous spearhead" (p 155) make. The lines do not appear to be any kind of recognizable weapon, but should be more accurately labeled as "indeterminate lines" (pp. 142-143). On the presence of other indeterminate lines in Cosquer, Clottes & Courtin comment, "When they cover animals or lie beneath them, we practically never know whether the super-impositions are random or express some meaning in relation to the identifiable depiction" (p. 142). In my view, this prudent statement should also be applied to those engraved lines labeled as weapons.

What has been identified as an engraved penis 12 centimeters in length with testicles is also present at Cosquer.

While not having personally examined this image on site, as access is restricted, after careful study of a color photograph of the depiction, (http://www.siksite.com/ACave4.htm) the following are my impressions. First, more photographs are required from differing perspectives to better determine the presence of testicles which are said to comprise the depiction but are not clearly apparent in the photograph studied. Quality photographs from differing perspectives can also assist in a better comprehension of the context in which the depiction was drawn. The urethra opening is unrealistically drawn extending through the entire head area of the reputed penis. After study of the depiction, it is also possible that the image could just as convincingly represent the vulva and upper abdomen of a female. Finally, it is possible that the engraving was made on a much later visit to the cave, near or after circa 13,000 BP. It is also possible that an oil lamp was used on a later visit that did not leave charcoal traces that could be accurately dated. The original entrance to Cosquer cave is currently under the water of the Mediterranean due to the rise of the sea that reached its present level by circa 2,700 BP. However, evidence suggests that the cave entrance was nearly eight meters above sea level until circa 6,500 BP and could still be easily entered even at this late date (p. 37).

More study of this depiction is needed. If found to be convincing, this image would be extremely rare and the only possible exception to my assertion, that there is a lack of evidence for male images in cave art prior to 13,000 BP.

The interpretation that there are a number of convincing depictions of male humans present in the cave art has little credibility as there is little artifact evidence to support the claim. In cave art, of those images that are considered to be male or anthropoid, the question has long ago been asked: “What are they when seen merely as figures? The hypothesis that the ‘Anthropoids,’ represent humans masked as animals is implausible since only a few of them really stand upright, and since the addition of a tail does not make an animal. They are just as unrecognizable as animals as they are as human beings” (Raphael, 1945, p. 15).

Lorblanchet (1989) argues that Paleolithic cave art was a focus by the artists on the "universal forces of creation." For the artists the "anthromorphs" represented a "voluntary denial of the human shape rather than a conceptual incapacity." The artists intentionally depersonalized themselves through the disguise of the "ever-present animal." The anthromorphs are "anti-portraits," an intention by the artists to avoid the "snare of individuality" and so likenesses were not made that would have "brought to mind particular members of the group" (p. 139).

Amusingly and presumably, Lorblanchet alludes to the intention of the artists to avoid a particular human depiction as it would somehow reduce the effectiveness of, distract from, or disrupt the focus of relating the animal images to the universal forces of nature. The artists were relating the animal images to the universal forces of creation, and somehow human images would interfere in this process. The human image would in a sense be an unnatural intrusion. While I agree that the artists were relating the animal images to a creative force of origin, my response to Lorblanchet's view is that it constitutes a vague and unconvincing explanation for the anthromorph figures.

In contrast to the naturalistic and detailed animal images of the cave art, the anthropomorphs or "images that have been interpreted as having human-like male characteristics," are said to be not drawn well. "One can assume that if they were ill drawn this was not from incompetence but intention, though one can only guess why this was done" (Sieveking, 1979, p. 46). When compared with the realism of the animal images, the male human figures are a "grotesque absurdity" and perhaps "some mysterious taboo on representing the human face...can explain this strange paradox" (Nougier, 1966, p. 584). Another explanation for this phenomenon is that, "the artists were capable of drawing the human figures as realistically as they drew animal figures...My feeling is that there was little need to feature drawings of humans, since real-life humans were present and actively participating" (Pfeiffer, 1982, p. 148).

In regard to the anthropomorphs, it is not acceptable just to settle for a "guess" as to why they were poorly drawn.

There is no credible evidence of a "taboo" regarding the representation of a human figure. Pfeiffer's view is also obscure; he thinks the artists' standard for representing life forms is whether or not the living form was present. He insists that since the animals were not immediately present, that there was some sort of "need" to depict them. Conversely, since humans were present during the making of the art, there was no "need" to portray them. Pfeiffer's view is not convincing as he offers no explanation of what this need might be. This view also does not satisfactorily explain why the so-called male humans were poorly drawn.

"Male figures in Upper Paleolithic art are known from engravings and paintings, but not from sculptures. Most of them are fantastic composite beings arising from the imaginative pairing of man and horned animal. A number of them are grotesque and enigmatic figures and rather carelessly engraved" (Gimbutas, 1989, p. 175). If imaginative, one can only ask why the figures may not just as well be animal images. Since the artists could realistically depict animal images, imagination is the most convincing explanation for these unrealistic depictions.

On the tendency of researchers to see human features of male sorcerers in some of the art images, Laming (1959) alludes to the perceptual process of anthropomorphism and the tendency for anthropocentrism and androcentrism as she remarks, "It is easy to see faces, especially human faces, in rock formations, branches, clouds, etc., and therefore it seems prudent to refrain from jumping to conclusions" (p. 84). Of what are said to be human faces in parietal art, only "one or two faces could pass as realistic," (Vialou, 1998, p. 87) and these cannot be convincingly identified to be either male or female (Leroi-Gourhan, 1967, p. 130).

The usually ambiguous images that have been interpreted as male human figures, on closer examination appear to be animals that have been anthropomorphized, perhaps as a result of the long term relationship with, familiarity with, and dependence upon the animal for food.

Speculatively, a possible subconscious intention for some of these anthropomorphized images might also be an inarticulate way of expressing the evolutionary awareness that through eating, the life of the animal is transformed into the life of the human through ingestion. Along this line of thinking, Conkey (1981) also mentions that the composite creatures having both human and animal features might represent the continuity between human and animal (p. 23).

Since a number of images appear to be intentionally distorted, for example the elongated “dachshund horses,” from Spain and the “distorted horses” from France, (Pfieffer, 1982, p. 139) and even multi-legged animals, (Laming, 1959, p. 72) these unusual figures also suggest the evolving capacity for creative imagination.

In conclusion, I have investigated the most well-known claims of the presence of male humans in images of Paleolithic cave art prior to circa 13,000 BP. In so doing I have reached the conclusion that the Paleolithic cave images known as the “sorcerer of Les Trois Freres,” the “sorcerer with bow” at Les Trois-Freres, the so-called “bird man” at Lascaux, and the “killed man” at Cosquer, as well as other figures identified as anthromorphs, can be better explained as the result of super-impositioning, anthropomorphized animals, or creative imagining.

The tendency by male researchers to perceive a number of the cave art images as hunters dressed in animal skins is also due to the biased influences of anthropocentrism, the considering of humans to be more important than other living or nonliving forms, and regarding and interpreting experience of the world in terms of human desires and interests; and androcentrism, the tendency to be concerned with or to emphasize male views or interests. Both of these cognitive tendencies through subconscious perception and conscious conception have played a role in erroneously identifying the above discussed images as male humans dressed or disguised as animals.

The absence of male images associated with cave art during the Paleolithic era prior to 13,000 BP contributes additional support to the petitionary-midwife theory, that there was prevalent during that time a general gynocentric orientation and that the cave artists were primarily females who probably in small family groups on occasion were assisted by gynocentrically oriented males.

Chapter 6

Female Figures

In this chapter I will argue that the Paleolithic female figures are an expression of a long enduring earth cultus or religion, and as such are related to the two other expressions of religion during the Middle and Upper Paleolithic era that I have explored, Neanderthal burial and cave art. The phenomena of burial and cave art are interactions with the earth, and the female figures are a symbolic expression of a human dependency on and interaction with the earth. I will establish evidence of this by determining the prominent characteristics of the female figures, and by investigating and critiquing the theories that seek to explain the meaning of the figures. I will show that while the overall shape of the figures resembles the human female form, lacking specific details such as facial features, realistic arms and hands, lower legs and feet, the depictions more accurately represent an anthropomorphism of the earth perceived to be the female-like origin of human, animal and plant life.

Whether engraved, painted, or portable sculptures, the female figures represent both an animistic and anthropomorphic perception and analogical conception of the earth to be the female origin of life; and, as such, are the earliest recognized image of a human deity. The term "Venus figure" is an anthropocentric misnomer, as the images should be more accurately referred to as "Earth figures." The planet earth was made knowable through anthropomorphizing it. Based on the artifact evidence, the female figures are a conceived combination of where Paleolithic humans observed they came from individually, the female body, and where life, on which they depended upon for sustenance originated, the mysterious interior of the earth.

There is a nearly complete lack of male portable sculpture dating to the Paleolithic era. At most, a few figures prior to circa 13,000 BP are accepted to be male, while identification of these is supported by only partial remains (Duhard, 1987; McDermott, 1996, p. 236; Marshack, 1996, p. 263).

The gender overwhelmingly represented in sculpted portable art during the Paleolithic era is the female. Fewer of these female figures are found in cave art as engravings, (La grotte de Cussac, 2001) as paintings, (Clottes et al., 2001, pp. 168-170) and as relief sculpture; the majority of the figures consist of portable art.

The name Venus as applied to the Paleolithic female figures has been used since the 1860's. The term "Venus impudique," meaning the immodest Venus, was used to describe an ivory female figure found in France, an allusion and contrast to the nude pose of classical statues of Venus, the goddess of love, in which she seeks to conceal her breasts and genital area (Witcombe, 1998).

Chronologically the female figures generally date from circa 30,000-12,000 BP (Neugebauer-Maresch, 1989; Delporte, 1993; Bosinski, 1991; Clottes et al., 2001, pp. 168-170). Geographically the female figures have been found over a large area extending from France to Russia, and from Germany to Italy. To date none has been found in Spain (Gamble, 1982, p. 96; McDermott, 1996, p. 232). There are approximately 100 female figures that date from circa 25,000-20,000 BP, (Vialou, 1998) while in all of the Upper Paleolithic era over 188 female figures have been found to date, (Rice, 1982, p. 402) and more continue to be found (La grotte de Cussac, 2001). The figures, ranging from hand-sized to just under a meter in length were variously engraved or carved from limestone, hematite, serpentine, antler, the ivory tusks of mammoths, and in a few cases fired clay (Dickson, 1990, pp. 100-103).

While there exist numerous female figures, my discussion will focus on three exemplars, those from Willendorf, Savignano, and Angles-sur-Anglin. The criterion for choosing these three particulars is to provide a range of geography, style, and time periods. The Willendorf is from Austria and dated to circa 26,000-24,000 BP; the Savignano is from Italy and dated to circa 25,000 BP; and the Angles-sur-Anglin figures are from France dated to circa 15,000 BP. The Willendorf and Savignano females are portable, while the Angles-sur-Anglin figurines are sculpted cave figures.

These three sculptures depict the general appearance of many of the female Earth figures, breasts, rounded abdomen, hips, and lack facial features and feet.

The female figure of Willendorf was found in 1908 in Austria, and today is located in the Naturhistorisches Museum in Vienna. Dated to circa 26,000-24,000 BP, the figurine is 11 centimeters in height, and made from limestone. It was found in an area of seven mammoth hunter campsites along with bone remains and other artifacts (Brandtner, 1993). For my research, I observed a reproduction of the Willendorf figure at the Museum of Natural History in New York during May 2000. While small, the sculpture is nonetheless impressive; and it is the most reproduced and well known of all the female figures. The Willendorf figure has no face. Instead, the facial area and head are marked by what is usually said to be seven rows or bands of plaited "hair" (Dickson, 1990, p. 101). Witcombe (1998) comments that it does not seem possible that hair could have been styled in this manner, and also observes that the figure is obese. The torso, including the breasts, abdomen, hips, and vulva, is the most emphasized area of the figure. The arms, just barely indicated, are unnaturally thin, and the hands are placed on the upper half of the breasts that have no nipples. What may be bracelets are suggested by markings on the wrists. The figure has no feet. Traces of red ochre were found on the figure (Brandtner, 1993). These features will be referred to and discussed in more detail.

The female figure of Savignano was discovered one meter underground near Modena, Italy in 1925 by workers on a building project; no other artifacts were located at the site. General agreement by scholars date the figure to circa 25,000 BP. The image was carved from greenish yellow serpentine stone and is 22 centimeters in height. The legs are joined and end in a point having no feet. The vulva or pubic triangle is apparent; the buttocks are prominently extended. The abdomen swells gently and there is a hint of the navel area.

On each side a realistic roll of adipose tissue is apparent. The breasts are prominent and asymmetrical, and just above there seems to be a clavicle ridge.

The upper arms are visible, but eventually fade into the forearms and breasts with no hands indicated. The head area is conical shaped and has no features except a vertical ridge that roughly bilaterally separates it, almost reminiscent of a nasal ridge (Graziosi, 1960, pp. 51-53). The form seems to flow from the stone. In this figure the head and face are even less emphasized and unnecessary. Here, as in other figures, it is the female form of the breasts, abdomen, hips, and vulva area that are most prominent.

While the majority of the female figures are portable and free-standing, some are not. One of the best known is the 42.5 centimeters high female figure of Laussel, carved using flint tools and dated to circa 22,000-20,000 BP (Witcombe, 1998). Discovered in 1911 in the Beune valley of France, not far from Lascaux, the site is located on a large ledge. The figure was found on a monumental block of stone fallen from the area above, and from which the depiction was eventually removed (Nougier, 1966, p. 590).

I have also chosen to discuss three interesting non-portable and less publicized female figures. These depictions dated to circa 15,000 BP were discovered during 1950-51 at the site of Angles-sur-Anglin in France. The figures were found at the base of a cliff alongside a stream in an area of several rock-shelters. Though not now apparent, there may also exist caves in the cliff base that are at present concealed by large rock falls (Breuil, 1979, p. 335).

Beneath the overhanging ledge of a rock-shelter on the wall surface, several intact animal figures of bison, horses, and ibex were found engraved or sculpted in low-relief. In the debris fallen from an area of the shelter walls were blocks of stone with the remains of painted and engraved animal images. A panel of three female figures approximately 150 centimeters in height was also found on the wall surface. The bodies have no head, shoulders, or arms; the suggestion of breasts on two of the figures, the curved bulge of the abdomen, waist, hips, vulva, and suggested engraved flat outline of legs without feet are depicted.

The female figure on the left still retains the visible outline of the upper and partial lower legs. The middle figure shows some evidence of deterioration of what was at one time a shaped outline of the upper and partial lower legs. The figure on the right shows part of the upper legs, and is superimposed upon two bison.

The figures were placed on the wall under an overhanging ledge that on first inspection seems too small for the upper half of the figures. However, the artists could have reduced the scale of the figures and easily had room enough to portray the complete female form. The lack of upper features on the figures suggests that the top of the body, the shoulders, neck and head were not depicted as these features were not as important. What was obviously important to the artists were the breasts abdomen, hips, and vulva, the significance of which will be discussed.

Theories for the Female Figures

It is generally agreed that for Upper Paleolithic humans the making of the female_figures was not a random act, but that they were made for a particular purpose (Delporte, 1993, p. 255). I will examine a number of the theories that explain what the artists' intention was for making the female figures.

The known archeological contexts for many of the female figures include the remains of living sites, near a hut, in pits, or in hearth areas (Gamble, 1982, p. 96). Since most of the female figures share a common style, seem to have been made for the intention of display, and have not been found associated with burials, Gamble thinks they contributed to conveying information among groups during population growth and environmental and social change during the Upper Paleolithic era (p. 98).

It is reasonable to assume that the female figures were made for a particular purpose, and that they served to inform others of a particular view or concept. Yet there exists no convincing evidence that the figures served primarily as a focus of information exchange among differing groups.

Perhaps due to the rapid and increasing use of computers, the information exchange theory has been in vogue during the last thirty years and as previously discussed has been unconvincingly offered as an explanation for cave art as well (Barton, Clark, & Cohen, 1994).

Harding (1976) argues that two of the female figures, including the Willendorf figurine, show evidence of the medical condition of "massive hypertrophy of the breasts," or in other words, excess mammary development. Both figures display excessive breast development, and the "bowed heads...may reflect the physical and psychological distress known to accompany the malady." This theory is based on the use of analogy of this malady with modern humans in African tribal groups, and while it is possible this condition might have existed during the Paleolithic era, there is no artifact evidence to support this view.

It has also been advocated that Paleolithic males, "could not live without predicting big game behavior and movements, or without a female companion, and this accounts for the intense preoccupation with both shown in Paleolithic art" (Geist, 1978, p. 308). While anxiety certainly would have existed concerning these areas of experience, Geist assumes the artists of the figurines were exclusively male. Realistically, both genders would have had intense concerns for food and a mate. The gender of the sculptors is unknown, yet it is generally assumed that males sculpted the female figures. But as Rice (1982) points out, there is no evidence for this assumption and it is just as likely that females were the sculptors (p. 412).

Soffer, Adovasio & Hyland (2000) do not think that there is one single meaning for the female figures. They also think that what was previously characterized as the plaited hair of the Willendorf and several other of the female figures, is actually a woven hat. Calling attention to the artifact remains of impressions found in clay fragments that appear to be baskets, nets, and cordage made of plant fiber circa 27,000 BP, Soffer et al. think that some of the features found on the Willendorf figure and a few other figures represent woven and plaited clothing that include hats and knotted hairnets or snoods, body bandeaux, belts, and one example of a string skirt.

Soffer et al. think the clothing was made by women, and that the wearing of the garments was a mark of social prestige and status; the fabrics were not for everyday wear, but were associated with ritual. The explanation offered for the absence of facial features on the female figures said to be wearing a cap or snood, is that "the social (as opposed to individual) importance of the headgear in Paleolithic ideology was far more important than portraying specific individual facial features" (p. 518).

In their article Soffer et al. admit that the Paleolithic female figures are "often unclad" (p. 515). Based upon 11 fairly complete female figures including the Willendorf, and what are said to be 10 female heads some of which do not appear identifiable as human females, and nine other abstract forms that only vaguely resemble a human being, Soffer et al. characterize these figures as wearing an article of clothing, such as a hat, bandeaux, or belt. They imply that these female figures served as models for the crafted clothing that were articles of prestige made and worn by women during the Paleolithic era.

In my view, what is said to be a headdress, belt, or bandeaux on a few of the figures, could be better explained as secondary decorative details applied to what are primarily and unquestionably nude female images. The argument that the lack of facial features on the female figures is the result of social importance while wearing what is said to be a cap or snood is also not convincing. I do agree with Soffer et al. that the images were most likely shaped by female artists. Yet it is also possible that at least some of the figures were made by gynocentrically oriented males.

Collins & Onians (1978) argue that the three main images portrayed during 33,000-23,000 BP are the vulvas, depicted alone or paired with partial animals on slabs of rock, animals, and female figures, and these indicate primary desires or needs for food and sex (pp. 14-15). Referring to the female figures, Onians thinks that no later culture gives so much prominence to such complete depictions of the fully nude female body (p. 11).

He thinks the female figures represent primary desires or needs for sex by adolescent males who were kept from physical access to the women by the older male relatives.

This frustration then contributed to the production of images of their youthful desire, the female figures. The young males projected their fantasies of sex onto the artistic images which provided substitute visual and tactile satisfaction (Collins & Onians, 1978, p. 21). While this group dynamic could have occurred, there is no evidence that this would have served as the intention for the figures. None of the figures appear in a sexually receptive or provocative posture, nor are any shown in the act of intercourse or in the company of males. This view is psychoanalytic in origin and also relies on analogical reasoning and comparison with historic tribal cultures.

Collins & Onians (1978) also point out that the bodily areas emphasized on the Willendorf as well as other figurines are the breasts, shoulders, abdomen, buttocks, and thighs, and that these areas are of most interest to males during love-making. In contrast, the lack of facial detail, undeveloped lower legs and feet, lower arms and hands, indicate a lack of interest during love-making (pp. 12-13). This is an amusing but unconvincing view. If the female figures were the result of a concern by males for love-making, then it would be reasonable to expect the vulva to be prominently displayed. However, Hadingham (1979) observes that while the vulva is marked on the Willendorf figure and others, this detail is more often missing from most female figures (p. 221).

Marshack (1991) theorizes that the female figures represent stories made up by early humans about feminine processes or experience relating to birth, death, lactation, and menstruation (p. 318). The red ochre painted on some of the female figures is also said to be a "symbolic and storied gesture" that "signified...the blood color of life" (p. 288). While I agree with Marshack on the significance of red ochre being symbolic of life, and accept the possibility that there were stories extant during the Upper Paleolithic era, there is just no artifact evidence of this.

Marshack draws much of the rationale for his views from the study of historic tribal groups, and then infers this was also the intention and meaning for Paleolithic humans.

Giedion (1962) thinks the female figures were idols of a mother cult and represented an ancestor from whom the group came into existence (p. 453). This view is based on comparison with historic cultures and is anthropocentric in that it proposes that the makers of the images were concerned only with human origin. In my view the figures are an answer to the question of where life came from, and further represent how the earth was perceived and conceived by early humans.

Since there are numerous figures with similar characteristics of large breasts, abdomen, hips, and lack of facial features and feet, Witcombe (1998) thinks there must have existed a shared understanding and meaning during the Paleolithic era. He thinks the figures represent an Earth mother or Mother goddess, and may indicate matriarchy, or rule by women. Dickson (1990) considers the female figurines to be the remains of a relatively short-lived religious cult, (p. 100) presumably associated with women. Maringer (1960) also thinks that the figures were the idols of a "great mother cult" that occurred during the Upper Paleolithic era (p. 160).

I generally agree with Witcombe that the figures represented a shared understanding and meaning and that this was associated with the earth as the female origin of existence. While there exists evidence of a gynocentric orientation during the Upper Paleolithic era, such as the use of red ochre in womb-like areas of the caves, and there is nearly a total lack of male images in cave and portable art, there are no artifacts that necessarily suggest matriarchy. I also agree with Dickson that the female figures are expressions of a religious view, but I would disagree that Paleolithic religious practice lasted only a short time. In my view the religious perception and conception of the interior of the earth as the origin of life and existence began with burial circa 100,000 BP, and includes the making of cave art that endured until circa 10,000. BP.

Maringer's view that the figures were the idols of a mother cult while generally correct, is vague and anthropocentrically misleading.

Murray (1963) thinks that prior to knowledge of the male contribution to reproduction that occurred only during the beginning of agriculture when men no longer hunted and began to spend more time in settled communities with women, the female was considered to be the sole cause of the newborn. She was the life-giver and the exclusive food-giver, yet how this process occurred was unknown to her (pp. 4-8). Based on her study of historical cultures, Murray hypothetically concludes it is quite common that a young girl during the Paleolithic era would have become a wife as early as her first menstruation, a mother at 11 or 12, and a grandmother by the age of 25 (p. 81). During the advanced stage of pregnancy and reduced activity, the condition of pregnancy would have occupied much of the expectant mother's thoughts. A group of pregnant women having the capacity of speech would have discussed their experiences of quickening and carrying the fetus within. They would have anticipated the pending event of childbirth, perhaps considering it to be an awesome as well as a painful and dangerous event (p. 68). Murray thinks that the importance and concern of pregnancy to women was then represented by the female figures which represented and served as a protective goddess of childbirth.

I agree with most of Murray's hypothetical view. The process of procreation was probably unknown to humans during most of the Paleolithic era, while young women more than likely would have borne children at an early age, and the condition of pregnancy must have been a topic of communication among women. However, I disagree with Murray as to what the female figures represent. While I agree the figures do represent the process of bringing forth life, they do not represent human pregnancy as much as they do an anthropomorphism of the earth.

Geist (1978) remarks that since the face, feet, and hands were not represented in the female figurines, these features might have been purposely obscured to conceal the identity of the male's mate from spirits during a religious ritual.

Individual identity was obscure because of fear that the spirit being beseeched during circumstances of anxiety would become malevolent (p. 325). This view is of course based on analogy with historic tribal groups, and there is no acceptable artifact evidence that this occurred during the Paleolithic era.

Giedon (1962) also suggests that the female figures are expressions of a fertility cult (p. 178). However, from study of contemporary tribal cultures, it has been pointed out by a number of researchers that these peoples are usually not aware of the relationship between sexual intercourse and birth (Collins & Onians, 1978, p. 12; Murray, 1963). While a number of researchers see evidence of a strong interest in sexuality in the female figurines, only a "few have the pubic triangle marked, and even fewer have the median cleft...these figures accentuate the breasts, buttocks and hips; they may represent fecundity but they do not draw attention to the vulva" (Bahn & Vertut, 1997, p. 187).

Rice's (1982) related view argues that the more than 200 female figures found to date represent a wide span of ages. Significantly, she points out that while a number of researchers perceive the figures as pregnant and so interpret them as a concern with fertility, most of the figurines do not appear to be pregnant, and none are shown in childbirth, nursing young, or with a child (p. 402). This is an important point. I also challenge the long held view that the female figures represent a concern with human fertility or are pregnant. I agree with Rice that the figures do not portray pregnancy, nor are any of the female figures depicted giving birth, nursing, or with children. No convincing figure of an infant or child has ever been found. There is no evidence of complimentary nude male figures that suggest a concern with human reproduction.

What has been said to be the most convincing evidence of a pregnant woman giving birth is the female figure of Monpazier which has the vulva and lower abdomen prominently displayed. The stone figure is a 55 mm high limonite or iron hydroxide conglomeration in the naturally occurring likeness of a human female having a head, breasts, torso, and a distended abdomen, buttocks, legs, and feet.

The head of the figure has two eyes roughly carved into it and the breast area was enhanced by the artist to appear more realistic. It also has what originally might have been a naturally occurring cavity in the conglomerate, but which has been intentionally shaped and enlarged into a more prominent, deep, and oval vulva opening (Marshack, 1996, pp. 260-263).

It has been argued by a gynecologist (Duhard, 1991, p. 553) that the figure is depicted in the condition of pregnancy. He states, “The Monpazier statuette is a pregnant woman with isolated posterior steatopygia” (p.559). The question is, how can a natural stone formation be said to be pregnant with enlarged buttocks when neither the abdomen nor the posterior have been shaped by a human artist? The figure can be more accurately described as a natural formation that was chosen for its resemblance to the condition of pregnancy and posterior enlargement. Gimbutas, (1989) a female researcher, comments that the figure is in the “preparturition” stage (p. 103). My response to both of these views is that they are anthropocentrically biased.

A better phenomenological approach to reality is to describe only what is observed. Granted, the figure suggests but does not actually depict an imminent human birth. Since the abdomen, buttocks, legs and feet, are in their natural unenhanced shape, the abdomen was not intentionally modified to depict a human pregnancy but only resembles this condition. The shape of the abdomen being coincidental, it was not the intention of the artist to portray a specific human pregnancy which is only suggested by the natural shape of the rock. Since the rock is a natural formation from the earth and only three areas, including the eyes, breasts, and vulva were enhanced to more closely resemble a human female, the figure primarily represents the earth and only secondarily a human female. The rock came from the earth, and being an integral part of it, and naturally resembling a human female, was further enhanced and anthropomorphized to symbolize the primary function of the earth, the giving of birth to animal and plant life.

The figure, like the other female sculptures, is an anthropomorphic symbol of the earth. Like women, the earth brought life into existence through an opening from its mysterious interior.

In all of the cave images there are no scenes of human activity or family life (Clottes & Lewis-Williams, 1998, p. 48). The female figures of cave art are usually portrayed as a single image, but more often are depicted in association with animals. The female figures of Angles-sur-Anglin in France are located on the wall surface beneath the overhanging ledge of a rock-shelter along with several animal figures of bison, horses, and ibex engraved or sculpted in low-relief. The female figure on the right has been superimposed upon two bison. At the recently discovered Paleolithic cave site of Cussac in France, tentatively dated to circa 22,000 BP, three engraved female images have been identified. One of them appears alone near a large cleft in the cave wall, while the other two are depicted on a panel of various animals (La grotte de Cussac, 2001). At Chauvet cave in France, what may be the oldest painting of a woman in the world was recently photographed and tentatively dated to circa 30,000 BP. The painting placed on an overhanging bulge of rock consists of what appears to be a female vulva placed between the elongated legs and bodies of a lion and bison. The image thus resembles the hips, vulva, and legs of a human female (Clottes et al., 2001, pp. 168-170).

The female figures do represent a concern with fertility, but not that of humans. Collins & Onians (1978) correctly point out that no culture other than the Paleolithic has given food animals such an important status in art (pp. 11, 14-15). Removing the anthropocentric biased view that the female figures are pregnant or represent a concern with human fertility, it becomes clear the figures can represent only one thing, a concern with the availability and origin of the animals. The figures are an anthropomorphic symbol of the earth that humans were subordinate to, dependent upon, and that they perceived and conceived to be the female-like origin of animal and plant life.

Rice (1982) thinks the female figures recognize or honor womanhood, and that Paleolithic females probably dominated the area of the home (p. 411).

While I agree with Rice that the female figures suggest Paleolithic humans were predominantly gynocentric, I disagree with her view that the figures were intended to honor womanhood. In my view, the reason none of the female figures are shown giving birth, suckling, or with a child, is that the figurines represent an anthropomorphism of the earth as the greater origin of life and existence.

McDermott (1996) describes the female figures as consisting mainly of hand-sized obese nude women having "faceless and usually down-turned heads, thin arms...voluminous and pendulous breasts, exaggeratedly large or elevated buttocks...a prominent, presumably pregnant or adipose abdomen with a large elliptical navel...oddly bent, unnaturally short tapering legs which terminate in either a rounded point or disproportionally small feet" (p. 228). While the overall shape is easily recognized, McDermott comments, "these anatomical details do not add up to an accurate image of the human figure" (p. 228). His explanation for this is that Upper Paleolithic women had concerns regarding their body, and so women made the Venus figures as a "form of self-portrait executed millennia before the invention of mirrors" (p. 245). The images served a materialist function as they preserved a record of physical changes and expressed the self-regard women had for their bodies. It is "the fixed angle of self-regard" that explains the realistic but unusual proportions of the body parts of the female figures. Viewing oneself that is, looking down at one's body while standing served as the self-model for the figures. McDermott photographed what modern women see as they look down upon their own bodies and then compared the photos with the female figures from the same perspective. He found the two perspectives matched.

McDermott does make a most important observation when he calls attention to the finding that circa 29,000-23,000 BP "a striking selectivity in gender exists" for the carved human figures, as "only one of the six figures long claimed as males in the literature for Palovian-Kostenkian-Gravettian or earlier levels can withstand even cursory scrutiny."

The important question he asks is, "If men were involved in creating human images at this time, why are virtually no males represented?" His answer is that it was women who "first developed human image making as accurate records of physical changes they alone experienced" (pp. 235, 247).

Leroi-Gourhan's (1967) findings support McDermott's assertion that there are virtually no male sculptures found in Paleolithic portable art: "Male figurines are so few they need only be mentioned...there is a fragment of a statuette which is apparently male....At Kostienki I, several heads in profile were discovered...the faces are stylized like animal heads, a convention which has frequently led to the statement that they represent men wearing animal masks" (p. 96).

I agree with McDermott that while the overall shape is easily recognized to be female, the anatomical details of being faceless, down-cast head, unusually thin arms, and unnatural short tapering legs that end in a round point or unusually small feet, do not add up to an accurate image of the human figure. However, I do not agree with his view that the figures represent a self-portrait as an expression of the self regard women had for their bodies as an explanation for the realistic but unusual bodily proportions of the female figures. My view is that the figures were not intended to portray human females, but instead were an anthropomorphism of the earth as the origin of life and existence. I also agree that since no convincing evidence of male figure sculptures have been discovered dating to the Upper Paleolithic era prior to 13,000 BP, and it is reasonable that if males were sculptors then male figures would be evident, then it is reasonable to accept that women were the sculptors of the female figures. However, it is possible that at least some of the female figures were also made by gynocentrically oriented males during this time.

Rudgley (1999) refers to the female figures as a "symbol of cosmological significance" for both "religious and practical knowledge...for the various forces of nature and the various aspects of culture" (pp. 199-200). While insightful, Rudgley's view is general, vague, and without explanation.

However, I do agree that the female figures are a cultural symbol that represent both a religious and practical cosmological view that is related to nature. The figures are an anthropomorphism of the earth as the preternatural origin of life. Perceiving the earth anthropomorphically also served as a practical explanation of its unknown shape.

For Markale (1999) the female figures represent an "ideology" or a "vision of divine femininity" regarding sexuality, yet the images do not refer so much to human sexuality, as they do to the "metaphysics of sex" (p. 58). Since the female figures may portray genitals but usually have no face, Markale thinks there is a "conscious desire not to represent precise individuality" (p. 59). Markale sees this to be the sculptor's "determination to locate no reference point upon the mystery of sexuality and procreation" (p. 59). The figures represent not a particular, but rather a general or universal. Markale claims that "the best hypothesis would be to see in these statuettes and engravings a representation of femininity as such, anonymous and universal, a symbolic form of the ineffable divine," that she refers to as being the "Goddess of the Beginnings" (p. 59).

I agree with Markale that the female figures represent an ideology regarding a concern for what is beyond individual human sexuality. The images are an ideational answer to a question posed by early humans: what larger presence has brought forth life into existence? I would agree that the figures are symbolic and represent a universal or greater origin of existence. However, the symbolic female figures are a reference not to an ineffable beginning, but refer to human interaction with the greater physical presence of the earth, and especially to its mysterious interior that like a womb brought forth animal and plant life.

Summary and Discussion

I will summarize so as to provide an overview for the continuity of sequence leading to the development of the female figures. I have defined religion as an effort to find the way back to the beginning, to reconnect to the origin of life.

The cognitive bases for religion in the Paleolithic era were the innate perceptual processes of animism, anthropomorphism, dreams, and rudimentary conceptual reasoning. These cognitive processes which are innate in human beings are evident in the expression of Neanderthal burials. Through observation of animal and plant life coming from its interior, and images of the deceased in dreams, the Neanderthals animistically and anthropomorphically perceived the earth to be the female-like origin of life. Intentionally placing the deceased and offerings in the interior of the earth where many forms of life were observed to come from, Neanderthals were practicing a religion.

The next stage in the development of Paleolithic era religion was the engraving and painting of cave art by Homo sapiens sapiens. Here the same innate cognitive processes of animism, anthropomorphism, dreams, and rudimentary reasoning continue to be apparent. Partial shapes resembling animals were animistically perceived in the cave surface, and the cave was anthropomorphized to be a female-like womb and the origin of animal and plant life. Vivid images of animals perceived in dreams were also likely associated with the darkness of the interior of the earth accessed through caves. The early human ability for rudimentary reasoning expressed these perceptual subconscious processes through conscious behavior. Based on the evidence of hand prints, footprints, and the colored dots found in the caves, the artists were primarily female who by enhancing natural features resembling animals, both assisted and petitioned the earth to bring forth or send the animals and plants to be hunted and gathered as food. The faunal-image anomaly provides support for the view that the artists were petitioning for what they did not have, the animal portrayed. The lack of images that can be convincingly identified as male in cave and sculpted portable art provides additional support for the view of a gynocentric orientation during the Paleolithic era circa 35,000-13,000 BP.

Burial and the making of cave art are interactions with the earth, and female figures are symbolic of this dependent and interactive primal relationship with the earth.

The behavioral expressions of burial and cave art are the practices of a religion, of perceiving the interior of the earth to be the origin of life. Through the cognitive processes of animism, anthropomorphism, and rudimentary reasoning, early humans perceived the interior of the earth to be the female-like origin of life. This comprehension in turn was expressed in the behavior of making the cave art and portable female figures.

I conclude that the essential meaning of the female figures consists of the following view which I have previously and partially presented during my investigative critique. The features that are generally emphasized in the female figures are the overall shape of the usually rotund body, and the enlarged rounded areas, such as the breasts, abdomen, and hips; areas that have been variously characterized as fat, adipose tissue, or as being pregnant. In general the female figures have few facial features such as eyes, nose, and mouth; the arms and hands are often negligibly present; and the feet are missing. While marked on the Willendorf, Angles-sur-Anglin figures and a few others, the vulvae are missing from many of the images. No nipples are indicated on the breasts, and the female figures are never depicted in actual childbirth, nursing newborns, with children and there are no scenes of human activity or family life. There is also little evidence of clothing, yet humans had to have worn clothing during the predominantly cooler and cold climate of the Upper Paleolithic.

These observations in toto prompt a question. Are these characteristics an accurate portrayal of the human female? The evidence suggests an emphatic no! Lacking these details, which the artists were quite capable of depicting, the female figures are generalized images representing an idea, not a particular identifiable human female.

The Angles-sur-Anglin female figures are a perceptual and rudimentary conceptual overlay imposed upon the earth. The behavioral expression of both portable and cave female figures represent how early humans comprehended what the earth was for them.

In general, the most emphasized bodily areas of the female figures are the breasts, abdomen, and hips including the buttocks and vulva. In the human psyche the female breasts were likely then as today associated with nourishment and the sustaining of life, while the abdomen is the area where the mystery of life began and developed, and the hip including the vulva, is where life first appeared and then exited from the body. Like the human female, the earth also provided nourishment, and animal and plant life were observed to come from within its greater interior.

The term "Venus figure" is an anthropocentric misdirected misnomer; the images should be more accurately referred to as Earth figures. The female figures are a perceptual anthropomorphism and analogical conception of the earliest recognized image of a human deity, the interior of the earth. The human figures are a conceived combination of where the artists knew they came from individually, the female body, and where animal and plant life, required for life sustenance originated, the mysterious interior of the earth upon which they lived.

The female figures are a way of thinking about and relating with the earth. They are the expression of an earth cultus or geocentric and gynocentric religious view that endured from 100,000 BP beginning with Neanderthal burial, continued through the development of cave art, and finally along with the cave depictions came to an abrupt end circa 10,000 BP. It is this ending of the making of the cave art and female figures that forms the topic of the final chapter discussion.

Chapter 7

Decline of Paleolithic Art and Religion

The artifact evidence confirms that distinct changes are apparent near the end of the Paleolithic era circa 13,000-10,000 BP. The practice of Neanderthal burial that had included placing offerings in the grave had come to an end as the species became extinct by circa 30,000 BP. However, after 35,000 BP in Europe, there is evidence of intentional burial and grave offerings by Homo sapiens sapiens (Harrold, 1980) that has continued to this day, with a possible brief decline of this behavior occurring circa 11,000-9,000 BP. The artifact evidence also confirms that circa 11,000 BP, the making of cave art came to an end, as did the sculpting of the female figures, circa 12,000 BP. The question to be asked here is, what event or events occurred during the period circa 13,000-10,000 BP that contributed to the decline of these phenomena?

In this section I will focus on the phenomenon of the sudden decline of Paleolithic cave art. I will examine the evidence, found in the Azilian culture located in southern France and in Levantine art from the area of eastern Spain that suggests a change of view occurred near the end of the Paleolithic era. I will seek to establish that during this time the view of the interior of the earth as the exclusive female origin of existence began to decline. The geocentric and gynocentric religious view of existence lasting through the Paleolithic era circa 100,000-10,000 BP was replaced by anthropocentric and androcentric orientations.

In Western Europe beginning circa 40,000-35,000 BP, there occurred what Mellars (1998) refers to as an "Upper Palaeolithic revolution" (p. 42). He comments that this revolution is evident in the overall increase of skill in stone tool making, the making and use of ornaments crafted of bone, antler, and ivory (pp. 49, 51-52, 66-67), and the making of cave and portable art (pp. 67-75). I agree with Mellars that there was a revolution in the areas of technology and art beginning circa 35,000 BP that continued until the end of the Paleolithic era circa 13,000-10,000 BP and beyond.

I attribute this gradual process of innovation to a steady increase and evolution of intelligence. As a result of evolving intelligence, as evidenced by such developments as the bow and arrow, the taming and eventual domestication of animals, and knowledge of plant growth from seed, Paleolithic humans also became aware of the male contribution to human reproduction.

The comprehension of procreation and the resulting change of view regarding the origin of existence was to result in the relatively rapid decline and abrupt end of cave art image-making and the sculpting of the nude female figures; and even the practice of burial was reduced during this time. The cessation of these artistic and behavioral expressions in turn signals the end of the Paleolithic era and furnishes an explanation for the end of the prevalent Paleolithic geocentric and gynocentric religious view.

Azilian Art

I will first investigate the phenomenon of Azilian art and the theories that seek to explain it. The era known as the Azilian was named after the site of Le Mas d' Azil in the French Pyrenees. The remains of this culture date to circa 11,000-9,000 BP. What is of interest in the Azilian culture is the abrupt disappearance of cave art. In place of the realistic images of cave art, there is found what appear to be meaningless abstract incisions on pieces of bone and stones (Bahn & Couraud, 1984, p. 156) and smooth mostly painted and some engraved pebbles. To date some 1,967 of these pebbles have been found, having 16 distinctive designs (Dickson, 1990, pp. 82-83).

The pebbles are flat, smooth, and oval-shaped quartzite, limestone, or usually blue schist obtained from the rivers, measuring 3-13 cm in length, to 6 cm in width, and 0.3-2.5 cm thick. Most of the designs have been painted with red ochre using some sort of a brush or finger, or incised with a sharp-edge tool, and were discovered at a total of 37 sites in Europe (Bahn & Couraud, 1984, p. 157). D'Errico (1992) mentions one site located in England (p. 95).

Location	Number of sites
France	28
Spain	5
Italy	3
Switzerland	1
England	1

It has been suggested that the designs might be a numerical system, possibly used to calculate moon cycles (Dickson, 1990, p. 84) and/or symbolize ritual ideas (Hadingham, 1979, p. 266). Maringer (1960) makes ethnographic comparisons with historic tribal groups in Australia and Tasmania, and thinks the Azilian designs are ancestor stones that represent deceased relatives. Maringer argues that some of the pebble designs are schematized human shapes. In contrasting seven of the 16 pebble designs with a number of human or anthropomorphic images from later Levantine art from Spain, Maringer finds a number of similarities (p. 178).

In his study of Azilian art, D'Errico (1992) used microscopic analysis to examine 146 incised pebbles from 25 sites mostly in France. He thinks that based on the handling and range of motion required to fashion the engravings, the designs were meaningful to the artists in some way. Microscopic analysis indicates that in many instances, the incisions of a pebble were all made by the same tool during a single series of operations. Since hunting tallies and lunar calendars would have been made over a relative long period of time, D'Errico rules out the possibility that the engraved pebbles were used for this purpose (p. 94). Despite a certain constancy of the engravings there appears to be no rigidity in the fashioning of the designs that would suggest ritual and therefore a sacral meaning. Both incised and painted pebbles display the use of a technical and cultural behavior learned through imitation or tradition (pp. 100-101). D'Errico (1992) concludes that the Azilians attributed a symbolic value to the engravings, and that at least some of the Azilian abstract designs are schematized depictions of humans and animals such as a bird and fish (pp. 105-106).

I agree with D'Errico that the designs were meaningful to the artists in some way and did not serve as hunting tallies and lunar calendars or have a religious significance. I agree with both Maringer and D'Errico that some of the images on the painted and engraved pebbles are schematized humans and animals.

It is obvious that the intention for art during the Azilian has completely changed. My understanding of this transition, from realistic animal figures on cave surfaces to abstract designs on small pebbles, is that the latter were not intended to be petitions to the earth. The pebble art does not suggest a transition to an improved mode of symbolic and intellectual expression, but rather represents a decline from the former realistic cave art that served as petitions to the earth perceived and conceived to be the origin of life and existence.

The artifact evidence of small hand prints, footprints, red and black dots, and the presence of young children and infants in the caves suggests the cave art was made primarily by women. However, there does not exist any convincing evidence to suggest which gender was primarily responsible for the Azilian art. Whether made by males, females, or both genders, the Azilian depictions are designs performed only as an enfeebled continuation of a formerly geocentric and gynocentric tradition.

Theories For The Change From Paleolithic To Azilian Art

To explain the change from Paleolithic art to Azilian art, Sieveking (1979) thinks that based on the long continuity of Upper Paleolithic art, that society was in a state of equilibrium during this time and experienced no significant social changes. This change is in contrast to the post-Paleolithic era when "habitat, subsistence and art all alter," and this she thinks was not the result of climate change which had to have occurred many times in the past (p. 206). The habitat change referred to by Sieveking occurs at the close of the last Ice Age. Prior to this a glacial period existed throughout much of northern Europe with fluctuations of warming and severe cold occurring 70,000-11,000 BP. The cold was severe circa 18,000 BP, but a warming trend occurred by 14,000 BP.

Glaciers melted and the present climate pattern began circa 11,000 BP (Smith, 1992, p. 6). The large herds of horses, reindeer, mammoth, and bison moved northward following the retreating glaciers. Tundra was replaced by forests of fir and pine, and later by birch, ash, and oak trees. In these woods, animals such as deer, boar, and ibex were more difficult to hunt.

Subsistence changed for the Azilian culture. Faunal evidence indicates these humans turned to the rivers and sea-shore for food, leaving behind middens or shell and bone mounds of discarded marine creatures. There was a dramatic increase in exploitation of marine life including fish and shellfish, and also a dramatic increase in bird and small game hunting (Binford, 1972, p. 425).

In Sieveking's (1979) view, the main cause for this change of subsistence as well as the end of Paleolithic art was triggered "by an expansion in population, such as we know to have occurred in the late Magdalenian....Naturalistic art declined under these conditions and caves received no further decoration" (pp. 206-207). Sieveking thinks that since the population was growing and the larger herd animals such as reindeer had moved further to the north, the only readily available protein was fish, shellfish, and small game. She implies that there was no need to draw animals, and so all deep cave art image-making was abruptly abandoned. However, her explanation is not convincing. Fish continued to be present in the streams and rivers and humans subsisted on them, but images of them were no longer depicted. Images of trout, salmon, and pike were drawn prior to 10,000 BP (Leroi-Gourhan, 1967, pp. 111, 408) but not after this time.

While most of the bone and flint tools made by the Azilians were smaller compared with those of previous generations, there was no uniform break with the past. In regard to the end of Paleolithic art, Hadingham (1979) points out that it is almost as if some kind of great spiritual, economic or social collapse occurred circa 11,000 BP. However, rather than a spiritual catastrophe, he thinks an economic and social collapse took place during this time.

Mainly as a result of the retreating glaciers, the reindeer, bison, and horses no longer migrated into Western Europe. This lack of a major economic food supply in turn led to a form of social collapse, since an increase in population was also occurring during this time (pp. 270-271).

There was surely a response and adjustment to the changing supply of game, yet life continued in the same manner of hunting-gathering. While the making of images within the caves ended abruptly, the making of art continued, though it's content and location drastically changed, confined mostly to painted and engraved pebbles. While Hadingham suggests a spiritual collapse might have contributed to the end of Paleolithic cave art, he does not venture to offer any thoughts on this view.

D'Errico (1992) argues that the change from the realistic cave art of the Paleolithic era to the schematic designs painted and engraved on pebbles during the Azilian was the result of a change of subsistence patterns.

"Some of the animals that were the source of the symbolic imaginary world of the Magdalenian artists died out or migrated towards the end of glaciation, but while this cannot but have had an effect on artistic manifestations it does not necessarily imply a shift towards abstraction. On the Spanish Atlantic...and Mediterranean coasts and in Italy, no important change in fauna can be observed between the Final Upper Paleolithic and the Epipaleolithic, but both the artistic manifestations and the stone and bone tool industries of these regions display the same trends as have been described for the French Azilian. Cultural evolution must therefore not be neglected" (pp. 105-106).

D'Errico makes a very good point here. While a change of subsistence would have had an effect on the animals portrayed, it does not satisfactorily explain the transition from realistic cave art to schematic designs on small pebbles. Also, since the fauna remained the same during this time in Spain and Italy, yet similar schematic art appears in these regions just as in France and other areas, then it is more likely that some sort of cultural or social change occurred over a wide area.

Sieveking, (1979) commenting on the extended duration of Paleolithic cave art, thinks that only a strong social sanction such as a religion would have been important enough to have been practiced for such a long time (p. 206). However, she does not relate a religious view with the demise of Paleolithic art. Instead she prefers the explanation of environmental change, population growth, and a change of subsistence as contributing to the transition to Azilian art.

I have discussed how the artifact evidence suggests that beginning circa 100,000 BP and continuing to circa 10,000 BP, there existed the longest lasting religious view of humankind. This geocentric and gynocentric orientation was that the interior of the earth was the female origin of existence; this religious view contributed to the intention for Neanderthal burial, the making of cave art, and the sculpting of female figures. Therefore I concur with Sieveking that a religious view contributed to the extended practice of cave art. While D'Errico favors a cultural change explanation, and both Hadingham and Sieveking at least mention the influence of a religious view as a possible contributing factor to the extended practice of and collapse of cave art, they are both silent as to artifact evidence. I will present evidence that suggests there was a collapse of a spiritual or religious view during this time, and that this collapse contributed to the rapid change from the realistic cave and sculpted female figure art of the Paleolithic era to the differing content of Azilian art.

End of the Paleolithic Religious View

After review of the artifacts and theories for the end of Paleolithic cave art that occurred circa 13,000-10,000 BP, I shall proceed by presenting findings that have led me to the essential meaning for this occurrence.

With the end of the Ice Age and retreating glaciers beginning circa 14,000 BP, the large herd animals of mammoth and reindeer were no longer prevalent.

Since in my view the animal images were drawn as petitions for the earth to bring them to life and to send them to be hunted for food; no matter how many images were drawn as petitions, the animals did not appear. In part, what contributed to the end of the making of deep cave art circa 13,000-10,000 BP, is that just as in any religion, if no assistance is rendered by the deity, then it will soon cease to be accepted and implored.

The artifact evidence suggests that sometime circa 13,000-10,000 BP, human males learned of their role in reproduction. D'Errico (1992) calls attention to some of the last Paleolithic cave art dating to circa 11,000 BP from the French caves of Fronsac, Font-Bargeix, and Gouy. The cave art of Fronsac and Font-Bargeix is described as having bovine and horse images. But more numerous than these animals are the images associated with humans, including not only vulvas, but also phalluses and outlines of the human shape. (See also Bosinski, 1991, p. 57) The images associated with humans actually outnumber and marginalize the animal images. Realistic cave animal depictions are found in Gouy cave, as are schematic animal images having a checkered pattern similar to the design found associated with some of the Azilian art. Referring to the cave art of these three late Paleolithic caves, D'Errico (1992) remarks, "We seem here, to be witnessing the transition from one artistic world to the other" (p. 106).

My view is that the content of the cave art of Fronsac and Font-Bargeix caves suggests an awareness of the interdependence of female and male genitals and most importantly the discovery of the male contribution to reproduction. During this time humans became aware that life began not just within and from the menstrual blood of the female body, but that it began only with the addition of another body fluid, male sperm. For long years it was likely accepted that only the mother and her menstrual blood formed or gave life to the young. However, it was eventually recognized that the sexual act and male sperm were essential for reproduction. My assertion is that this comprehension occurred circa 13,000-10,000 BP.

Prior to this realization, what Paleolithic males were probably thought to contribute to existence was not the beginning of human life but rather assistance in maintaining it. This contribution principally consisted of making stone and wood tools and weapons, shelters, and having the physical strength for aggression to hunt and defend group members against predators and possible other human enemies. Prior to circa 13,000 BP males were probably thought of as only capable of killing life, not bringing it into existence. However, increasing cognitive ability and observation led to the recognition of the male contribution to reproduction. Humans, and especially males, circa 13,000-10,000 BP, became aware that the lack of sex and male sperm meant a lack of pregnancy.

Gimbutas (1982) asserts that no evidence exists from Neolithic times that humans had an understanding of biological conception (p. 237). However, other researchers have advocated that knowledge of physical paternity probably occurred during the Neolithic as a result of keeping livestock and agriculture (Barton, 1940, p. 139; Murray, 1963, pp. 4-8). I agree with Barton and Murray, and place the awareness of the male contribution to reproduction even further back in time to the last of the Paleolithic era circa 13,000-10,000 BP.

The artifact evidence suggests that during the Paleolithic era the young of various animals were captured, tamed, and some eventually domesticated, and that it was through the observation of tamed animals that the male contribution to reproduction was discovered. An increase in settlement lifestyle most likely contributed to the capturing of the young of animals such as horses and the semi-domestication of them. Horse teeth have been found at the Neanderthal site of La Quina and the Upper Paleolithic site of Le Placard, both located in France. At both sites several horse teeth were found that show evidence of wear patterns associated with crib-biting, a phenomenon found in modern horses as a result of boredom and confinement. If these findings can be confirmed, it will show that at least at some sites horses were tethered for extended periods (Bahn, 1980).

There is evidence that horses were tamed by the late Paleolithic era (Burkitt, 1972, pp. 56-57). Engraved on a hyoid bone found at the Azilian site of Le Mas d' Azil in the Pyrenees, and dated to 12,000 BP, is an image of a horse head that shows the presence of a halter (Ruspoli, 1986, p. 21). The horse head is engraved on both sides of the bone that is 4.6 centimeters long. The eye, nose, mouth, and hair are clearly portrayed, as well as what is plainly a rope halter incised on the image. Ropes were being made and used by this time. The impression from a lump of clay showing the remains of a braided three-strand rope made of plant fibers and dated to circa 14,000 BP was discovered in the Lascaux cave in France (White, 1986, p. 49; Soffer et al., 2000, p. 817). The actual remains of a rope consisting of three pieces of twisted plant fiber has also recently been found in Israel dating to 19,300 BP (Anthropology News, 2000).

The process of domestication has been defined as the separation of a breeding population from its wild predecessors (Davis & Valla, 1978, p.608). The dog was one of the first domesticated animals. In the Palegawra cave in Iran, canine fossil remains have been found similar to the modern dog. In a grave excavated in modern Israel, dating slightly later than circa 10,000 BP, the skeleton of a young boy was found holding the remains of a young canine (Angela & Angela, 1993, pp. 272-273). The remains of a dog dated to circa 10,000 BP were identified from the state of Idaho in the United States (Davis & Valla, 1978, p.608).

Through DNA research it has been confirmed that wolves were the ancestors of the domesticated dog, and that circa 15,000-10,000 BP there was a distinct morphological change from wolf to the dog line. This would have occurred as a result of the human transition from a hunting-gathering to a more sedentary and agricultural lifestyle, at which time selective breeding became more intensive (Vila et al., 1999). It is likely that from observing the mating and the rather short period of gestation in dogs, approximately 62 days, the male contribution to procreation was discovered during this time.

Having a subsistence lifestyle of foraging as well as hunting, eventually led to a developed knowledge of food plants including roots, mushrooms, berries, and fruits. Based upon long observation of plants through foraging, humans during the Upper Paleolithic era eventually acquired the rudimentary knowledge that only when seeds were placed into the soil from above did they grow from within the earth (Blumler & Byrne, 1991; Pringle, 1998b).

Through the observation of tamed and domesticated animals and an increasing knowledge of plants, humans eventually comprehended that only when the male human or animal placed semen into the female did she give birth to young, and only when a seed was placed into the ground did life come into existence from within the earth. The contributing factors for the coming into existence of life was recognized to be "semen and seeds." Following this discovery, humans no longer engraved or painted the animal and plant images, as petitions to the earth to bring forth living forms.

There is more evidence for the male realization regarding the contribution to reproduction. Phallic images appear frequently in late Paleolithic art (Vialou, 1998, p. 77) but not prior to this time. It is significant that phallic images have been found dating near the end of the Paleolithic era in France and Spain, and in the Mid-East circa 12,000 BP. Marshack (1997) presents evidence of three convincing carved phallic images. One is a carved reindeer antler from Montastruc, France, dating to circa 13,000 BP. Another from the Mideast dating to circa 13,000-11,000 BP, is a natural flint having a phallic shape, incised with lines indicating the testicles, foreskin, and urethra opening. A third limestone phallus dating to circa 11,000 BP from the Fazael site in Israel, clearly shows the foreskin groove and slit (p. 81). Several other bone and antler phallic forms have been discovered dating to circa 13,000-10,000 BP (Leroi-Gourhan, 1967, pp. 60, 500). Only from this time is it possible to find the presence of males expressed in Paleolithic art.

A survey of human representation in the Upper Paleolithic seems to show, as we move from epoch to epoch, that the correlation and proportion of male to female figures is wholly reversed.

In the earliest period, statuettes and low reliefs of women are fairly numerous, then they grow scarce, giving way to abbreviated figures or signs. On the other hand, complete representations of men are rare in the early periods, and much more frequent in the caves during the peak period of the interior sanctuaries (Leroi-Gourhan, 1967, p. 123). While the phrase "much more frequent" is debatable, there is more evidence of male presence in the caves and the art during the peak period of the Paleolithic era which would have been circa 12,000-10,000 BP.

It has been assumed that the caves were the entire domain of men throughout the Upper Paleolithic era. But the only scenes which can convincingly be said to contain small spears, missiles, or darts thrown, or wounded animals, originate only circa 13,000-10,000 BP, and generally coincide with the ending of cave art circa 12,000-10,000 BP.

There has been a recent claim for the depiction of weapons on wounded animals at Cosquer cave discovered in 1991 in the south of France. Here visits by early humans have been carbon-dated to circa 26,000-19,000 BP (Clottes & Courtin, 1996, p. 31). While not a thorough study of all the engraved lines at Cosquer, the research reports 28 depictions of animals in association with 46 long and elongated lines. Of these lines 24 are long single lines and 22 are labeled as "feathered and/or barbed" lines. Of the 22 "feathered lines, 18 of them are forked or "Y-shaped" while the other four are forked or Y-shaped at one end and "barbed" at the other (p. 148-149). These "feathered and/or barbed" lines occur on only 14 of the animals (p. 144-145) out of a total of 100 depictions (p. 123).

After examining the artifacts, my view is that there is no convincing evidence of weapons in the cave art of Cosquer. The researchers list two categories and three possible types of weapons present at Cosquer. These are listed as feathered and barbed lines (pp. 144-145, 152) that are said to be depictions of either arrow, spear, or harpoon projectile weapons (p. 156). The interpretation of these engraved lines as feathered or barbed weapons is not convincing.

At least four of the depictions (pp. 73, 122, 141, 144) resemble those convincingly identified by Marshack (1991) as plants. They even have what appear to be roots on them as well. Other feathered or barbed lines may also be either plants or partial super-impositioned and incomplete animal depictions (Clottes & Courtin, 1996, pp. 94, 112-113, 132).

Clottes & Courtin also accept a third category of engraved lines they refer to as "indeterminate lines." The lines categorized as indeterminate include, "spots of paint, straight or curved lines, scraped strips, and lines of all sorts" (p. 143). These indeterminate lines cannot reasonably be said to represent anything recognizable. Pertaining to the indeterminate lines the comment is made that, "When they cover animals or lie beneath them, we practically never know whether the superimpositions are random or express some meaning in relation to the identifiable depiction" (p. 142). This prudent statement should also be applied to the forked lines that are designated as "feathered or barbed" projectile weapons.

Clottes & Courtin suggest that the depictions in Cosquer cave were drawn by hunters who sought to depict the wounding of some of the animals. They remark, "it is best to see in these signs depictions of projectile weapons which in the larger context of the great hunt in which Paleolithic art occurs, is not surprising" (p. 152). However, since approximately only 14 percent of the animal images are claimed to have "feathered" or "barbed" projectile weapons engraved on them, this begs the question. What can be said for the remaining and overwhelming 86 percent that have no lines on them identified as weapons? What can be the explanation; could it be they were not hunted?

Clottes & Courtin state that the forked and straight lines which intersect the depictions "at times" were found to have been "engraved *before* the animal" (p. 150). In these instances the evidence is convincing that the artists did not intend the lines to be projectile weapons thrown or shot at the animal.

Since the "feathered and/or barbed" lines occur on only 14 percent of the animals (p. 144-145) the finding that some of these forked lines which intersect them were engraved prior to the image, would at least in these instances further lower the number of depictions which it is claimed show evidence of projectile weapons.

Even Clottes & Courtin acknowledge that if the forked lines were drawn by the artists to represent weapons, the location of them "on the body of the animals was of little importance, since they touch indiscriminately the head, the back, the underbelly, the flank, and the fore- and hindquarters" (p. 150). The lines said to be weapons are not drawn aimed for vital areas that would realistically ensure that the animal would be efficiently killed. Forked lines can be also be observed to be randomly positioned on the cave wall and not located on an animal depiction (pp. 145,150, 169).

Clottes & Courtin comment that the engraved lines they interpret as projectile weapons could have been made by the artists either in a "real or metaphorical way" (p. 150). What an amusing and silly statement. That the forked line lines were a metaphor or symbol for a representation of a weapon is a poor and unconvincing argument, and they are not even close to being realistic. These supposed "metaphorical weapons" can be compared with the more realistic depiction of weapons on the animals such as those at Niaux (Clottes & Courtin 1996, p. 164; Graziosi, 1960, figs. 207-210).

There is also said to be a single "sign in the form of an arrow with a loop at the base" that has "hit a seal at the edge of the hindquarters" (pp. 121, 131, 133, 144). Considering the position of the triangular shape in relation to the body of the seal, it is not actually positioned on the animal but in conjunction with it, and it is not convincing that it was meant to portray harm to the animal. Further, if the image was intended by the artist to be either an arrow, spear, or harpoon, since the shaft appears to be flexible and looped at the end, it would hardly have served as an effective weapon to be shot or thrown. There are two engraved triangular arrow-like shapes that occur as part of another depiction of random curved and branched lines (pp. 145, 150).

There are also at least 11 triangular shapes located on a roughly rectangular depiction (p. 147). Aside from the triangular shapes, there are a number of other geometric shapes including zigzags, X-shaped crosses, a circle, a diamond, and rectangular shapes (pp. 144, 147, 150).

It is more convincing to view the forked and straight lines that intersect with a minority of animals as being indeterminate lines and/or as partial or unfinished superimposed depictions. Some are convincing images of plants. The cave art presented by Clottes & Courtin from Cosquer cave as evidence for the presence of male artists who were depicting hunting weapons and wounded animals circa 26,000-19,000 BP is not convincing or acceptable.

An acceptable and convincing example of hunting art is a bison drawn on the clay floor of the French cave at Niaux, a site at which some of the images have been radio-carbon dated to circa 13,000 BP. The original image was drawn around a natural cupule that served as the eye, and other cupules are located on the body, and the animal shows no alarm or indication of being wounded. At a later date incised marks resembling arrows or short spears were drawn around the body cupules so as to suggest wounds on the animal (Bahn & Vertut, 1997, p. 110). Several other cave images at Niaux, including bison and a horse, also show what appears to be incised and painted arrow or spear-like marks on them (Clottes & Courtin 1996, p. 164; Graziosi, 1960, figs. 207-210).

There is ample evidence by the end of the Paleolithic era and beginning of the Mesolithic era circa 10,000 BP, that the flints made and used were more geometric and the bow and arrow is wide-spread (Binford, 1972, p. 425). From the pelvic remains of a female skeleton buried and dating to circa 13,000 BP in Italy, a fragment of flint arrowhead was found. An arrowhead found lodged in the vertebra of a buried child, also in Italy dates from the same time (Bahn, 1997). A large number of stone-tip wood arrows have been found in several camps of reindeer hunters that date from circa 10,000 BP (Prideaux, 1973, p. 77).

The two oldest recognizable bow artifacts have been excavated in Denmark and date from circa 8,000 BP (Bahn, 1997). There are also many images of bows and arrows evident in later Levantine art.

When Paleolithic humans realized the life of animals did not come from the perceived partial resemblances of them swelling forth from the rock surface deep within caves, but that reproduction was due to the swelling of the penis and emission of sperm from the male human and animal, images as petitions to the earth as the origin of life were no longer engraved or painted. No longer was there a gynocentric concern for the origin of life below and within the earth. Life came not from below, but from the male above the female. When early males realized the relationship between the swelling of the penis, discharge of semen during intercourse, and the eventual swelling pregnancy of the female, there was a transformation of awareness and increase of androcentric values. No longer was woman the primary life-giver, but rather the recipient of the life-stuff of male semen.

When awareness of the male role in procreation occurred, there was no longer a need for women midwives to trek into the caves to engrave and paint the animal and plant images so as to assist the earth to give birth to them. There was no more need to enter into the caves, as the earth that was previously perceived and conceptualized as female ceased to be regarded as the exclusive origin of existence. The interior of the earth as the first anthropomorphic deity of human existence faded into oblivion.

Just as cave art was no longer made as petitions to the earth as the origin of life, and as the Earth female figures were not made any more, there is evidence that suggests burial as a return to the place of the origin of life drastically decreased for a time during the Azilian culture. Since a number of researchers agree there was an increase in population during the last of the Paleolithic era, (Sieveking, 1979, pp. 206-207; Hadingham, 1979, pp. 270-271) there should be an evident increase in the number of burials as well.

Dickson (1990) points out that burials circa 16,000-11,000 BP "are far more common than those of earlier periods." However, during the Azilian era circa 11,000-9,000 BP, burials are rare and only two of them have been adequately documented, the one located in France and the other in Spain (pp. 82-83; Tresguerres, 1976). Chamberlain (1997) observes that in England as elsewhere "Mesolithic burials are rare" and that beginning circa 8,000 BP and lasting until 6,000 BP few burials have been found. The phenomenon of a scarcity of burials during the Azilian and Mesolithic suggests that for a time the bodies were no longer interred. My view of the essential meaning of this phenomenon is that the earth was no longer perceived and conceived as the exclusive female origin of life, and so the body was no longer placed there at the time of death. Of course burial did continue after this time, but was probably based more on tradition and other factors rather than perceiving the earth to be the female origin of existence.

Levantine Art

Following the brief expression of Azilian art from circa 11,000-9,000 BP, there was a transition to what is known as Levantine art. Predominantly located in north and central eastern Spain, Levantine art was first discovered in 1903 and roughly spans the time period circa 9,000-6,000 BP.

Since the expressions of Paleolithic, Azilian, and Levantine art are geographically and sequentially related, contrasting the characteristics of Paleolithic art with Levantine art serves to further comprehension of the intention and meaning for the change from the former style to the latter. Of the Paleolithic cave art of Altamira, Spain, dated to circa 13,000 BP, it has been observed that, "Altimira painters have exploited the uneven nature of the rock, combining their colour with that of the rock, which confers on their works a natural intensity. The animals are not simply attached to the wall, coloured pictures on stone, but seem to be born from the stone, to live in terms of the material" (Moulin, 1965, p. 38).

These characteristics are then contrasted with the Mesolithic and Neolithic Levantine art of eastern Spain; "…the paintings of the Spanish Levant never reached the dimensions of those in the Magdalenian sanctuaries...figures are shown in two dimensions... adopting a linear outline and flat tints of red brown and sometimes black...This is essentially a graphic manner of portrayal; the paintings are spread out upon a surface of the…stone, they do not 'work' it, or exploit the material" (p. 46).

My explanation for this difference in style is that, for Paleolithic artists the inchoate animal shapes images were animistically perceived as actually coming from within the earth, and the act of enhancing by engraving and painting the images were a petitionary assistance to the origin of existence to bring forth the portrayed life forms. In contrast, Levantine art is two-dimensional on flat surfaces. The images are on stone but do not appear to be coming from or to be an intricate part of the natural surface, and therefore the images were not intended as petitions to the earth.

The Levantine artists lived in groups of about 100 individuals (Pericot, 1966, p. 210). Among the many paintings none depict a settlement or a permanent dwelling, yet the sense of a shared community is conveyed in the scenes (Prideaux, 1973, p. 150). For the first time in human existence the art depicts males, females, and a child in social relationships (p. 145). In Levantine art there are "far fewer paintings of women than of men" (Beltran, 1982, p. 46) and in contrast to the usual nudity of males, the women are almost never depicted nude. However, women's breasts are usually exposed and they are shown wearing skirts (p. 205).

According to latest count there are more than 700 sites of Levantine rock art dating from circa 10,000-6,000 BP. The most used color for the images is red ochre followed by black, and some white. The images are an average of 10-30 centimeters in size, while others are smaller and the largest is 120 centimeters high. In this art humans are the most numerous figures, followed by animals, and then geometric designs.

Male archers are the most frequently drawn images, while bovines and deer are the second most common figures. The most frequent behavior depicted is hunting, followed by scenes of conflict between groups of archers, and also executions of individuals struck with arrows. Domestic scenes include seated figures, one image of a woman walking with a child, a male and females dancing, the gathering of honey, and a few depictions of what appears to be a dog (Iberian Rock Art, 1999).

In contrast with most of Paleolithic art being located in the darkness of caves, Levantine art is placed in the open areas of shallow rock-shelters, overlooking sunlit vistas (Pfeiffer, 1982, pp. 149). In Paleolithic art beginning circa 13,000 BP, the few animals portrayed as wounded do not exhibit any indication of alarm or suffering. In Paleolithic art humans and animals are not portrayed in relationship to each other. The art does not depict hunting, the hunter, or the hunted animal, nor are any realistic recognizable objects such as weapons or tools portrayed (Vialou, 1998, pp. 84-87). However, in Levantine art the wounded animals are often portrayed with open mouths and collapsing legs that indicate the animal is in distress. The question has to be asked, "what changes in lifestyle occurred at that time to make artists include the suffering of wounded animals in more of their paintings" (Pfeiffer, 1982, p. 151).

One explanation for the change of the content of the art, including humans replacing animals as the main focus, is that over the span of the 35,000 years the Paleolithic era humans had evolved a "sense of self-confidence" (Prideaux, 1973, p. 145). This view suggests that over the course of human development there was an increase in intellectual or cognitive ability that resulted in more success in adapting to the environment and perhaps an increase in self-awareness. This view may suffice as a general explanation, but it does not explore the conditions for the change in the content of the art.

In my view the change in lifestyle and painting style was the result of a change of perception and conception as well as a change of artist gender.

No longer was the interior of the earth gynocentrically perceived and conceived to be the exclusive origin of life and existence. Since female images dominate almost the entire Upper Paleolithic era in the form of vulvas, prevalence of small hand prints, and sculpted female Earth figures, the artists depicting these images were primarily female, or at the very least the culture was gynocentrically oriented. There were no male images present, or convincing evidence of a male presence in cave art until the late Paleolithic circa 13,000 BP. The scenes of Levantine art consist predominantly of males, many with the phallus prominently displayed, (Prideaux, 1973) the hunting and killing of animals, group conflict, wounded individuals, and executions. It is reasonable to conclude that the artists were predominantly male and that the culture was androcentrically oriented during this time. Finally, testosterone had triumphed.

In Paleolithic art humans make up only three to four per cent of the images and these are almost exclusively female, while in Levantine art the number of human images is more than 28 percent of the total. Of approximately 3,000 human images in Levantine art, only one appears to be a child and pregnant females are not portrayed. The majority of images consists of males either hunting or in conflict. There is here a profound shift in the basic nature of art and its intention. One could easily conclude along with Pfeiffer (1982) that this was the art of hunters who enjoyed hunting (pp. 151-152).

In an excellent study, Boado & Romero (1993) compare Paleolithic art and the post-glacial Levantine art of eastern Spain by investigating the concepts of time and space expressed in the depictions. There are clear differences between the two styles, that of Paleolithic era art from circa 33,000-10,000 BP, and that of Levantine art circa 10,000-6,000 BP. The basic contrast between the two art styles is that in Paleolithic art the animals depicted are not those eaten as found in the fauna or food remains, while in Levantine art in general, the animals depicted do correspond with the fauna (pp. 187-189).

This is an important point that supports the petitionary-midwife model.

Unlike the Paleolithic cave images which were petitions (to the animistically and anthropomorphically perceived earth as the origin of life) for what was desired for food in the future, the Levantine images suggest the recording of actual past events and so portray stories. The Levantine faunal remains match those animals portrayed in the art.

Other contrasts are also noted. Paleolithic art is located deep inside caves, in darkness where torches or lamps are needed. There are no human figures or representations of their activities. The images are naturalistic, three dimensional, and utilize natural elements of the rock surface. There is no narrative; the images are portrayed as static or immobile and atemporal.

In contrast, Levantine art is located in open air sites and daylight. There are human figures performing various activities. The art is schematic, two dimensional, and does not make use of natural features of the rock surface. It is narrative, portrayed in temporal succession and displays a sequence of events in a specific time (p. 190). The art is a recording of events either remembered or storied.

Paleolithic Art	Levantine Art
Animals are the main focus.	Humans are the main focus.
Humans/animals not in relationship.	Humans/animals are in relationship.
No hunters or hunting scenes.	Hunters and hunting scenes.
Few animals are marked with unrealistic weapons, and show no fear or distress.	Hunted animals are in distress, and have realistic weapons
Animals depicted not found in fauna.	Animals depicted found in fauna
Located deep inside caves and darkness.	Located in open sites, daylight.
No human figures or activities.	Human figures and activities.

Naturalistic three dimensional images.	Schematic and two dimensional images.
Static, immobile, no time sequence.	Mobile, narrative time sequence.

In Paleolithic art human figures are three to four percent of the total figures versus Levantine art in which human figures are 28 percent of the total images. Paleolithic art does not depict the everyday world, while Levantine art is a social art where the drama of human activity is depicted. Boado & Romero conclude that “the two art forms are immersed in cognitive systems which possess totally distinct concepts of space and time” (pp. 191-192).

Paleolithic art is not concerned with humans and daily social life but with animals and plants. Space is not defined and there is no expression of time or sequence. In contrast, Levantine art shows that humans have a participating role in the environment and are concerned with daily social life; space is defined and there is a sequence of events portrayed in time. The art is also related to hunting strategies and to early animal domestication (pp. 197-198). The contrast of Upper Paleolithic art with Levantine art suggests a transition from a gynocentric and geocentric view of existence to an androcentric and anthropocentric view. Unlike the Paleolithic images of animals and plants directed to the earth as petitions, Levantine art is directed to other human beings as a record or story of mostly male events that include hunting and conflict. Using Marshack’s (1991) term, the images are “storied.”

Gimbutas observes that there is a continuation of regard for the human female from the Paleolithic into the Neolithic era circa 8,500-5,500 BP. However, after many years of research she concludes that during this time the “Great Goddess...is not the Earth, but a female human, capable of transforming herself into many living shapes,” such as “the bird, snake, or vegetation goddess” (p. 236). This relevant observation suggests that while drastically reduced, a gynocentric orientation was retained, but there was a move away from geocentricism that was soon replaced by more of an anthropocentric view.

During this time the human female is identified not so much with the interior of the earth but with the various observed ways associated with coming into existence, such as hatching bird eggs, the unusual rejuvenation via the shedding of the serpent skin, and the growth of plants and trees that bear grain, fruit and vegetables. While the cave and interior of the earth below was no longer perceived as the origin of existence, at least the fecundity of the soil above like the female continued to be revered. Just like the soil, the human or animal female was necessary to receive the seed from above.

In conclusion, evidence found in both Azilian and Levantine art suggests that a perceptual and conceptual change of view occurred near the end of the Paleolithic era circa 13,000-10,000 BP. During and after this time there is convincing evidence that suggests the geocentric and gynocentric view of existence was replaced by anthropocentrism and androcentrism, and as a consequence the interior of the earth was no longer considered by humans to be the exclusive female origin of life. Primarily as a result of an evolving intelligence as evidenced in the taming and eventual domestication of animals, an increasing knowledge of plants and the beginning of horticulture, and technological development such as the bow and arrow, the male contribution to both human and animal reproduction became known. The presence of phallic images in the cave art of the French caves of Fronsac and Font-Bargeix, and the sculpted phallic shapes from France and the Mideast circa 12,000-10,000 BP also strongly suggest a developing interest in and knowledge of the male contribution to reproduction. This awareness and change of view regarding the origin of life primarily resulted in the relatively rapid decline and abrupt end of cave art image-making, and the sculpting of the female Earth figures. The evidence also suggests that the practice of burial, as a behavior of placing the deceased where the origin of life was observed and perceived to come from, was reduced and discontinued for at least two thousand years. The end of these artistic and behavioral expressions circa 10,000 BP provides convincing evidence for the end of the Paleolithic animistic, anthropomorphic, and analogical religious view that the interior of the earth was the female-like origin of life.

Conclusion

For this study I have defined religion as the human effort to find and to reconnect to the origin of life and the environment. While the problem of the definition of religion has not been completely resolved, a significant contribution has been made in the direction of comprehending the basic or essential meaning of the term. I have limited my research for evidence of the first expression of religion to the Paleolithic era. Based on my definition of religion, I find convincing evidence of a religious view and practice during the Paleolithic era circa 100,000-10,000 BP. Paleolithic humans developed a religious view through sensory observation, the innate perceptual processes of animism, anthropomorphism, and dreams, and the conceptual process of rudimentary analogical reasoning.

A religion consists of cognitive processes that are expressed through various repetitive behaviors or rituals. Religious behavior is evident in the Paleolithic era artifacts of the non-utilitarian behaviors of intentional burial and the placing of grave offerings therein, in the making of cave art, and in the sculpted and engraved female figures. These repeated behaviors were evidently important; they occurred over immense periods of time within the span of circa 100,000-10,000 BP. In my view, the artifact remains of intentional Neanderthal burial, cave art, and the female figurines are expressions of religious thinking and behavior as a concern by early humans for the origin of life.

Throughout this study I have discussed the cognitive tendencies of contemporary researchers which have often contributed to the misunderstanding of Paleolithic era artifacts. One faulty method used by researchers to derive the meaning of prehistoric Paleolithic era artifacts is the use of analogy, comparing and relating them to what is known of historic cultures. Anthropocentrism and androcentrism have also contributed to erroneous interpretations of Paleolithic artifacts. The effect of these cognitive tendencies has contributed to not recognizing early burial to be the expression of the Neanderthal animistic perception that the interior of the earth was the origin of life and existence.

Anthropocentrism and androcentrism have also made it difficult to comprehend cave art to be petitions to the earth as the origin of animal and plant life; and the female figurines have traditionally been anthropocentrically labeled as "Venus" figures as an allusion to classical sculpture rather than referring to them more accurately to be anthropomorphized planet "Earth" figures. Researcher's over-reliance on the faculty of reasoning has also fragmented the continuum of the expressive behaviors (of Neanderthal burial, the making of cave art, and the sculpting of female figures) into disparate and discrete phenomena.

Recognizing the influence of these cognitive tendencies makes it easier to discern the essential meaning of Neanderthal burial, cave art, and female figures, to be expressions of attention and behavior directed to the earth. These triune phenomena are more accurately related parts of a whole. Each of these behavioral expressions shows evidence of sharing the same cognitive processes of animism, anthropomorphism, dreams, and rudimentary analogical reasoning. Each is the expression of Paleolithic humans' intimate relationship with the interior of the earth, perceived and conceived by them to be the origin of life.

There is convincing evidence of intentional burial by Neanderthals. Grave offerings ritually placed with the deceased, such as the flowers in the Shanidar IV site remains and the flint tools, red ochre, and curios of jasper and quartz found in the La Chapelle and Nahr Ibrahim remains, all placed on, beneath, and around the body, offer compelling evidence for intentional Neanderthal burials.

Neanderthals attained a rudimentary level of cognitive ability for symbolic thought, as evidenced by having a brain similar to Homo sapiens sapiens, the use of speech, the skilled technical ability for the Levallois method of stone-working, the ability to anticipate and predict the movement of game animals thereby planning where and when to move, and the making of non-utilitarian objects such as a shaped mammoth tooth coated with ochre, and zigzag and geometric designs.

These behavioral artifacts offer convincing evidence of Neanderthal intelligence and the ability for rudimentary reasoning and use of symbols. Based on this evidence, I conclude that they also had the ability for a rudimentary religious view.

When Neanderthals experienced physical death, there must have been a strong poignant desire to remedy or reverse the situation. Experiencing helplessness when death occurred, they could do little. The living could not bring the deceased back to life, no matter what might have been done to the body. An answer could have been to somehow place the child or adult back into the female human body from where it had originated, thereby restoring life and giving birth to the deceased again. Of course this was not possible. The only emotionally effective behavior was to protectively place the lifeless form where it was observed that much of life, like den-dwelling animals such as bears, insects, and plants originated from, and that was the interior of the earth. Through the innate psychological processes of animism, anthropomorphism, dreams, and rudimentary analogical reasoning, the earth was perceived and conceived to be the origin of life. Therefore burial was the rudimentary expression of a religious view, an earth cultus.

Like burial, cave art is also an expression of an earth cultus or geocentric and gynocentric religion. Paleolithic cave art represents a meaningful interaction with the earth. For Paleolithic era humans, the answer to the question of the origin of life was not metaphysical but physical. When Homo sapiens sapiens (who also buried their dead) sought to solve the mystery of the beginning of life and especially where the animals they depended on for food came from, they focused attention on the interior of the earth as an explanation. Through the cognitive processes of animism, anthropomorphism, and dreams, Paleolithic era humans perceived, and then through rudimentary reasoning conceived, that life came from a living origin and not from impersonal conditions of cause and effect and the matrix of the environment. The beginning of existence had to be living to bring forth life.

It also had to be visible and physical rather than invisible and non-physical, and it had to be personal or person-like. The gender of choice to express this conception was not male but rather the human female and the mystery within her that could bring life into existence. The mysterious ability of the female to bring forth life from within her body was equated with the equally mysterious greater interior of the earth. Plants, animals, and humans were not observed to be born from what was above or a visible or invisible beyond, but rather from within the earth and the mother. Life was experienced to come from within, out into existence. Vegetation came from within the soil below, and animal young came from within the mother while deep within the dens of the earth.

I have argued that the animal and occasional plant images were engraved and painted primarily but not exclusively by female midwives as petitions and assistance to the earth to bring forth the animals and plants into existence. It was through the innate subconscious perceptual processes of animism, anthropomorphism, and dreams, and rudimentary conscious reasoning that humans perceived and then conceived the earth to be a living female that brought forth all things from the interior of her body. Observing the partial resemblance of an animal shape in the cave surfaces, through these cognitive processes early humans gynocentrically perceived that the earth was giving birth to them. The unusual bulging, elongated, and flowing formations found in many caves bolstered the early human animistic view of the cave as a place of shaping, forming, and coming into existence. The cave was anthropomorphized to be a human-like womb, and areas coated with red ochre symbolized menstrual blood and the coming into existence of life. Dreams are a subconscious perceptual function, and the perceived vivid images of animals during sleep also inspired humans to make the cave art.

The prevalence of small hand prints and footprints, colored dots, and the presence of children and infants in the art caves suggest the artists were primarily women accompanied by their children.

The cave artists were primarily women along with gynocentrically oriented males who, by drawing the images based on the memory of sensory observation or perceived dream images, acted as midwives in petitioning and assisting the earth to give birth and life to animals and plants. The engravings and paintings represent petitions, primarily by women midwives, to the earth to give birth to or send the desired animal to provide food. Portraying the animal and plant images was also an assistance to the interior of the earth, considered to be the origin of life, so that it would eventually give birth and send or provide the animals and plants to be hunted and gathered. The red and black dots often found in association with the hand prints and animal images, and that mark the beginning and end of the location of the parietal depictions, are symbolic of fresh and dried drops of blood shed during menstruation.

The petitionary-midwife model also explains an anomaly in the faunal record, the contrast between animals depicted in the cave art and the remains of the animals eaten by the inhabitants. This phenomenon supports the petitionary view that the Paleolithic artists were asking for what was insufficient, the animals portrayed. The engraved and painted animal and plant images were petitions directed to the earth as the origin of life. Cave art is an expression of an earth cultus, a geocentric and gynocentric religion.

In spite of the attempt by Breuil and later researchers to identify some of the images portrayed in Paleolithic art as being male humans, there is no creditable evidence of this until after circa 13,000 BP. In some of the last expressions of Paleolithic cave art dating to circa 11,000 BP, phallic images have been found in the French caves of Fronsac and Font-Bargeix. Only during this time was the presence of males expressed in art. The cave images dated to circa 15,000 BP known as the "sorcerer of Les Trois Freres," the "sorcerer with bow" at Les Trois-Freres, the so-called "bird man" at Lascaux dated to circa 18,000 BP, and the "killed man" at Cosquer circa 26,000-19,000 BP, as well as a number of other anthromorph figures, are all better explained as the result of super-impositioning, anthropomorphized animals, and creative imagination on the part of the artists.

The tendency by contemporary researchers to perceive a number of cave art images as male hunters dressed in animal skins is also due to the biased cognitive influences of anthropocentrism and androcentrism. Both of these cognitive tendencies have contributed to erroneously identifying certain images as being male humans dressed or disguised as animals. The finding of a masculine presence in the cave art was necessary to support the views by early researchers that the making of the depictions was performed exclusively by male hunters or shamans.

For early humans, the female figurines had nothing to do with the planet Venus nor with classical sculpture. The female figures are the earliest anthropomorphism of a deity, the interior of the planet Earth as the maternal beginning of life. Since the Earth brought forth animal and plant life, humans perceived it animistically to be alive, perceived it anthropomorphically and conceived it analogically to be human-like, and therefore visually represented it as a female human form. The female figures were a perceptual and conceptual strategy to comprehend the earth. It was neither flat nor round, but rather it was comprehended to be the great living human-like female and mother origin of existence that brought forth and life and thereby provided nourishment.

Archeological evidence of the transition from the Paleolithic geocentric and gynocentric view of existence to an anthropocentric and androcentric orientation can be found dating from circa 13,000-6,000 BP in late Magdalenian, Azilian and Levantine art. During this time there is compelling evidence that the long-term geocentric and gynocentric Paleolithic view of existence was replaced by a Neolithic anthropocentric and androcentric view, and as a consequence the interior of the earth was no longer considered to be the exclusive female origin of existence. As a result of an evolving intelligence, evidence of which is found in the taming and eventual domestication of animals, the beginning of horticulture, and the technological development of the bow and arrow, humans became aware of the male contribution to reproduction. Of the tamed and domesticated animals, horses and dogs were most likely the species that contributed to an awareness of the human male's contribution to reproduction.

The presence of phallic images in the art of the French caves of Fronsac and Font-Bargeix, and the sculpted phallic shapes from France and the Mideast all dating to circa 13,000-10,000 BP, offer compelling evidence for human interest in and knowledge of reproduction at this time. Awareness of reproduction and the origin of life resulted in the relatively rapid decline and abrupt end of cave art image-making and the sculpting of the female Earth figures.

Since human population increased during the late Paleolithic era, there should be a corresponding increase in the number of burials during this time. However, there is evidence requiring further in-depth research that suggests the practice of burial was reduced or discontinued circa 11,000-9,000 BP. The geocentric and gynocentric view of the origin of existence predominated from approximately 100,000-13,000 BP. Taking 30 years to be a generation, within the brief period of 100 generations or 3,000 years circa 13,000-10,000 BP, the knowledge of the male contribution to reproduction had been realized throughout the Upper Paleolithic European population, sufficient to bring about the demise of the making of cave art and the nude female Earth figures.

Azilian art dates from circa 11,000-9,000 BP and is painted and engraved on pebbles. It is not possible at this time to attribute a primary gender for this artistic expression. Azilian art is either an enfeebled non-petitionary continuation of a long traditional artistic impulse by female artists, or it is the fledgling effort toward depiction made primarily by male artists. Whether made by males, females, or both genders, the Azilian depictions are designs made only as an enfeebled continuation of a formerly geocentric and gynocentric tradition. In Levantine art circa 9,000-6,000 BP, the most prevalent gender depicted is male, usually shown hunting, engaging in conflict, and with the phallus prominently displayed. The content of Levantine art suggests an androcentric orientation and that the gender of the artists was primarily male.

Since the end of the Paleolithic era 10,000 years ago, human perception, conception, and behavior, has not changed as drastically as might be expected.

The formative cognitive processes and expressive behaviors of the first practice of religion that began 100,000 years ago are still present. Today the practice of burial, art, and petitionary requests to a deity, and representations of the earth continue to exist. However, instead of sprinkled with ochre, the deceased individual may be laid to rest within the red fabric lining of a coffin, often along with personal offerings, and then placed within the earth. Instead of entering caves to commune with and petition the origin of existence through engraved or brightly colored paintings of animals and plants, there is entry into the enclosure of a temple building, there to marvel at the colored images, sculptures, or designs that serve to direct attention and petitions to a non-visible yet still animated and anthropomorphized male deity. This constructed holy enclosure became a substitute for the sacred female interior of the cave and earth of long ago. Within the holy enclosure attention is directed to an invisible male presence who first created, placed, or made life. While the planet environment continues to be referred to as Mother Nature or Mother Earth, in place of stone female figures painted with red ochre that anthropomorphize the earth, today globes are constructed with the oceans, continents, and countries colorfully portrayed on them.

It is evident that Paleolithic humans were survival oriented and observant of the terrain, climate, and animal and plant life, and that they sensed some super-animating presence that ever moved a changing environment and the growth of living forms. Early humans localized the animating force of life in the interior caves of the earth and anthropomorphized it to be a greater female mother of life. Paleolithic humans were generally correct to perceive the earth as the supportive and animating origin of their existence, as the modern theory of evolution has confirmed. The prehistoric perception of a super animating force is correct but a conceived anthropomorphic or human-like mother origin is not correct.

The German philosopher Arthur Schopenhauer (1788-1860) wrote the words, “Religions are the offspring of ignorance who do not long survive their mother.” Ignorance is the mother of religion as humans utilize human attributes to identify the origin of existence.

Anthropomorphic religions are based on ignorance, including any and all of the polytheistic and monotheistic variety.

Through long evolving time the human subconscious and conscious cognitive need to relate to the origin of the environment and life, produced the conception of human attributes that are reassuring to humans. The conception of a human-like female earth was the first religion that lasted from circa 100,000-10,000 BP. Circa 4,000 BP began a transition to polytheism and visibly crafted both female and male gods, and eventually in modern times developed a monotheistic nonvisible human-like male god. Modern theistic religions continue to incorrectly conceive of the origin of life as human-like and therefore the attribution error continues. In contrast, historically recent super animistic and non-anthropomorphic religions such as the Hindu view of Brahman, the Chinese Tao, and Buddhism are smaller than and not as popular as are larger anthropomorphic religions.

A religion is obviously not mathematical or scientific, therefore it is strictly an artistic expression. While both religion and art surely had a long covert background, the two phenomena both appeared nearly simultaneously and overtly in Paleolithic Europe. Therefore, in reality they are the same creative impulse, art as the external visual craft of engraving, painting, and sculpture, and religion as an internal artistic and conceptual creative way to identify and relate to where life came from by utilizing human attributes.

References

Abrahamian, L. H., Adams, K. M., Bahn, P. & Black, L. T. (1987). Comments. Current Anthropology, 28 (1), 71-85.

Anati, E. (1993). World rock art the primordial language. Valcamonica, Italia: Edizioni Del Centro.

Anthropology News Briefs. [On-line]. Available: http:// realindy.com / anthronews.htm

Angela, P. & Angela, A. (1993). The extraordinary story of human origins. (Trans. Gabriele Tonne). Buffalo, NY: Prometheus Books.

Bahn, P. (1998). Chauvet cave. In D. Vialou, Prehistoric Art and Civilization (pp. 138-139). New York: Harry N. Abrams.

Bahn, P. G. (1998). Neanderthals emancipated. Nature, 394 (6695), 719-721.

Bahn, P. (1997). Palaeolithic archers? Archaeology Newsbriefs,50 (3). [On-line]. Available:http://www.archaeology.org/9705 / newsbriefs/archers.html

Bahn, P. G. (1997). Dancing in the dark: Probing the phenomenon of Pleistocene cave art. BAR InternationalSeries, 667, 35-37.

Bahn, P. (1980). Crib-biting: Tethered horses in the Palaeolithic? World Archaeology, 12(2), 212-217.

Bahn, P. G. (1978). Water mythology and the distribution of Palaeolithic parietal art. Proceedings of the Prehistoric Society, 44, 125-134.

Bahn, P. G., & Couraud, C. (1984). Azilian pebbles: An unsolved mystery. Endeavor, 8(4), 156-158.

Bahn, P. G., & Vertut, J. (1997). Journey through the ice ages. Berkeley, CA: University of California.

Balter, M. (1995). Did Homo erectus tame fire first? Science, 268, 1570.

Balter, M. (1996). Cave structure boosts Neanderthal image. Science, 271 (5248), 449.

Balter, M. (2000). Paintings in Italian cave may be the oldest. Science, 290 (5491), 419, 421.

Bar-Yosef, O. (1997). Symbolic expressions in later prehistory of the Levant: Why are they so few? In M. W. Conkey (Ed.) Beyond art: Pleistocene image and symbol. (pp. 161-187).

San Francisco: California Academy of Sciences.

Bar-Yosef, O. & Callander, J. (1999). The women from Tabun: Garrod's doubts in historical perspective. Journal of Human Evolution, 37(6), 879-885.

Barham, L. (1999). From art and tools came human origins. British Archaeology, 42. [On-line]. Available:http: // www.britarch.ac.uk/ba/ba42feat.html

Barriere, C. (1976). L' Art de la Grotte de Gargas(i). (W. A. Drapkin, Trans.). Oxford, England: BAR Supplementary Series.

Barriere, C. (1984). Grotte de Gargas. In L' Art des Cavernes: Atlas des Grottes Ornees Paleolithiques Francaises (pp. 514-522).Paris, France: Imprimerie Nationale.

Barton, C. G. & Clark, A. Cohen. (1994). Art as information: explaining Upper Palaeolithic art in western Europe. World Archaeology, 26 (2), 185-207.

Barton, G. A. (1940). The Palaeolithic beginnings of religion—an interpretation. Proceedings of the American Philosophical Society, 82(2), 131-149.

Begley, S. (1999). Secrets of the cave' art. Newsweek.com: Science and Tecnology. [On-line]. Available:http:// www.newsweek.com/nw-rv/printed/us/st/sc01211. htm

Beltran, A. (1982). Rock art of the Spanish Levant. London: Cambridge University Press.

Binford, L. R. (1972). An archaeological perspective. New York: Seminar Press.

Binford, S. R. (1968). A structural comparison of disposal of the dead in the Mousterian and the upper Paleolithic. Southwestern Journal of Anthropology, 24 (2), 139-154.

Blanc, A. C. (1966). Some evidence for the ideologies of early man. In S. L Washburn (Ed.), Social life of earlyman (pp. 119-36). Chicago: Aldine Publishing.

Blumler, M. A. & Byrne, R. (1991). The ecological genetics of domestication and the origins of agriculture. Current Anthropology, 32(1), 23-35.

Boado, F.C. & Romero, R. P. (1993). Art, time and thought: a formal study comparing Paleolithic and postglacial art. World Archaeology, 25 (2), 187-203.

Bosinski, G. (1991). The representation of female figures in the Rhineland Magdalenian. Proceedings of the Prehistoric Society, 57(1), 51-64.

Bower, B. (1996). Visions on the rocks. Science News, 150(14), 216-217.

Bower, B. (1996). Whole-brain interpreter. Science News, 149, 124-125.

Brandtner, F. (1993). Die geschichte der Venus. [On-line]. Available:http://www.members.theglobe.com/fixado76/ges hven.htm

Breuil, H. (1979). Four hundred centuries of cave art. New York: Hacker Books.

Brockway, R.W. (1978). Neanderthal religion. Studies in religion, 7 (3), 317-321.

Broglio, A. (1999). Neanderthals and modern humans in Europe: Behavioural aspects. [On- line].Available:http://www.ivs la.unive.it/istituto/Convegni/Origini/Broglio.htm

Brown, S. J. (2001). Neanderthals and modern humans in western Europe. [On-line].Available:http://www.neanderthal-modern. com/weeurope.htm

Bulkeley, K. (1997). An introduction to the psychology of dreaming. Westport, CT: Praeger.

Bunge, M. (1962). Intuition and science. Englewood Cliffs, NJ: Prentice-Hall.

Burkitt, M. C. (1972). Our early ancestors. New York: Benjamin Blom.

Campbell, J. (1987). The masks of god:Primitive mythology. New York: Penguin.

Casino, B. J. (1999). Defining religion in American law. [On-line]. Available: http://www. Religiousfreedom.com/articles/ casino. htm

Chamberlain, A. (1997). In this dark place thy burying place. British Archaeology(26). [On-line]. Available: http://www. britarch. ac.uk/ba/ba26/ba26feat.html

Chase, P. G. & Dibble, H. L. (1987). Middle Paleolithic symbolism: a review of current evidence and interpretations. Journal of Anthropological Archaeo- logy, 6 (3), 263-296.

Chiron, C. Jambaque, I., Nabbout, R. Lounes, R., Syrota, A. &

Dulac, O. (1997). The right brain hemisphere is dominant in human infants. Brain, 120 (6), 1057-1065.

Clark, W. H. (1977). Handbook of parapsychology. In B. B. Wolman (Ed.), Parapsychology and religion(pp. 769-780). Jefferson, NC: McFarland &Company.

Clottes, J. (1989). The identification of human and animal figures in European Paleolithic art. (M. Conkey, Trans.). In H. Murphy (Ed.), Animals Into Art (pp. 21-56). London: Unwin Hyman.

Clottes, J. (1997). Art of the light and art of the depths. In M. W. Conkey (Ed.) Beyond art: Pleistocene image and symbol. (pp.203-215). San Francisco: California Academy of Sciences.

Clottes, J. (1998). New laboratory techniques and their impact on Paleolithic cave art. In Takeru Akazawa, Kenichi Aoki & Ofer Bar-Yosef (Eds.), Neanderthals and modern humans in western Asia (pp. 37-52). New York: Plenum Press.

Clottes, J. (2001). Paleolithic Europe. In D. S. Whitley (Ed.), Handbook of rock art research (pp. 459-481). Walnut Creek, CA: Altamira Press.

Clottes, J., Arnold, M., Aujoulat, N., Baffier, D., Debard, E., Delannoy, J. J., Evin, J., Feruglio, V., Fosse, P., Ferrier, C., Fritz, C., Garcia, M. A., Gely, B., Geneste, J. M., Girard, M., Guerin, C., Kervazo, B. Guillou, Y. L., Maksud, F., Morel, P. Oberlin, C., Packer, C., Perrette, Y., Philippe, M., Lamblin, J. R., Rouzaud, F., Schefer, J. L., Tisnerat, N., Tosello, G., & Valladas, Helene. (2001). La grotte Chauvet, l'art des origines. Paris: Editions du Seuil.

Clottes, J, & Courtin, J. (1996). The cave beneath the sea: Paleolithic images at Cosquer. (M. Garner, Trans.) New York: Harry N. Abrams.

Clottes, J, & Courtin, J. (1998). Cosquer cave. In D. Vialou, Prehistoric Art and Civilization (pp. 134-137). New York: Harry N. Abrams.

Clottes, J. & Lewis-Williams, D. (1998). The shamans of prehistory. New York: Harry N. Abrams.

Clottes, J., Courtin, J., Collina-Girard, J., Arnold, M., & Valladas, H. (1997). News from Cosquer cave: Climate studies, recording, sampling, dates. Antiquity, 71(272), 321-326.

Collins, D. & Onians, J. (1978). The origins of art. Art History, 1(1), 1-25.

Conkey, M. W. (1981). A century of Palaeolithic cave art. Archaeology, 34(94), 20- 28.

Conkey, M. W. (1983). On the origins of Paleolithic art: a review and some critical thoughts. BAR International Series, 164, 201-227.

Conkey, M. W. (1997). Mobilizing ideologies. In L. D. Hager (Ed.), Women in human evolution. (pp. 172-207). London: Routledge.

Constable, G. (1973). The Neanderthals. New York: Time-Life.

Davenport, D. & Jochim, M. A. (1988). The scene in the shaft at Lascaux. Antiquity, 62, 558-562.

Davidson, I. (1997). The power of pictures. In M. W. Conkey (Ed.), Beyond art: Pleistocene image and symbol. (pp. 125-159). San Francisco: California Academy of Sciences.

Davis, S. J. M. & Valla, F. R. (1978). Evidence for domestication of the dog 12,000 years ago in the Natufian of Israel. Nature, 276, pp. 608-610.

Delporte, H. (1993). Gravettian female figurines: A regional survey. In Heidi Knecht, Anne Pike-Tay & Randell White (Eds.), Before Lascaux, the Complex Record of the Early Upper Paleolithic (pp. 243-257). Boca Raton, FL: CRC Press.

Dennell, R. (1997). The world's oldest spears. Nature, 385(6619), 767-768.

D'Errico, F., Henshilwood, C., & Nilssen, P. (2001). An engraved bone fragment from c. 70,000-year-old Middle Stone Age levels at Blombos Cave, South Africa: Implications for the origin of symbolism and language. Antiquity, 75(288), 309-318.

D'Errico, F. (1992). Technology, motion, and the meaning of Epipaleolithic art. Current Anthropology, 33(1), 94-109.

Dibble, H. L. & Chase, P. G. (1993). On Mousterian and Natufian burials in the Levant. Current Anthropology, 34(2), 170-172.

Dickson, D. B. (1990). The dawn of belief. Tucson, AZ: University of Arizona Press.

Ducasse, C. J. (1953). A philosophical scrutiny of religion. New York: The Ronald Press.

Duhard, J. P. (1987). Edouard Piette avait raison: La "figurine a la ceinture" de Brassempouy est bien un homme. Bulletin S. A. S. O. 22, 207-212.

Duhard, J. P. (1991). The shape of Pleistocene women. Antiquity, 65(248), 552-561.

Dune, B. J. (1997). Subjectivity and intuition in the scientific method. In R. Davis-Floyd & P. S. Arvidson (Eds.), Intuition: The inside story (pp. 19-37). New York: Routledge.

Durkheim, E. (1965). The elementary forms of the religious life. (J. W. Swain, Trans.). New York: The Free Press.

Eaton, R. L. (1978). The evolution of trophy hunting. Carnivore,1, 110-121.

Eliade, M. (1959). The myth of the eternal return:Or cosmos and history. (W. R. Trask, Trans.). New York: Harper Torch-books.

Eliade, M. (1959). The myth of the eternal return. (W.R. Trask, Trans.). New York: Harcourt, Brace & World.

Eliade, M (1963). Patterns in comparative religion. (R. Sheed, Trans.). New York: Meridian Books.

Eliade, M. (1969). The quest: History and meaning in religion. Chicago: University of Chicago.

Eliade, M. (1978). A history of religious ideas. (Vol. 1). Chicago: University of Chicago.

Eliade, M. (1987). The encyclopedia of religion. (Vol. 2). New York: Macmillan.

Eliade, M. (1988). Autobiography. Vol. II. (M. L. Rickets, Trans.). Chicago: University of Chicago.

Feuerbach, L. (1873). The essence of religion. (A. Loos, Trans.). New York: Asa K. Butts & Company.

Feuerbach, L. (1957). The essence of Christianity. New York: Harper Torchbooks.

Frake, C. O. (1994). Dials: A study in the physical representation of cognitive systems. In C. Renfrew & E. Zubrow (Eds.), The ancient mind:Elements of cognitive archaeology (pp. 119-32). Great Britain: Cambridge University Press.

Frazer, J. G. (1951). The golden bough,a study in magic and religion. (Vol. 1). London: Macmillan.

Freud, S. (1961). The future of an illusion. (J. Strachey, Trans.). London: Hogarth Press.

Gamble, C. (1982). Interaction and alliance in Palaeolithic society. Man, 17 (1), 92-107.

Gargett, R. H. (1989). Grave shortcomings, the evidence for Neanderthal burial: Comments. Current Anthropology, 30 (2), 157-190.

Garrod, D. A. E. & Bate, D. M. A. (1937). The stone age of Mount Carmel. (Vol. 1). London: Oxford University Press.

Geertz, C. (1973). The interpretation of cultures. New York: Basic Books.

Geist, V. (1978). Life strategies, human evolution, environmental design. New York: Springer-Verlag.

Gibbons, A. (1998). Ancient island tools suggest Homo erectus was a seafarer. Science, 279 (5357), 1635-1637.

Giedion, S. (1962). The beginnings of art. New York: Bollingen Foundation.

Gimbutas, M. (1989). The language of the goddess. San Francisco: Harper.

Gimbutas, M. (1982). The goddesses and gods of old Europe. Los Angles: University of California Press.

Gombrich, E. H. (1977). Art and illusion: A study in the psychology of pictorial representation. London: Phaidon.

Gore, R. (1997). The dawn of humans. National Geographic, 191(5), 98-112.

Graziosi, P. (1960). Palaeolithic art. London: Faber and Faber.

Gutherie, S. E. (1993). Faces in the clouds, a new theory of religion. New York: Oxford University Press.

Hadingham, E. (1979). Secrets of the ice age. New York: Walker.

Halverson, J. (1987). Art for art's sake in the Paleolithic. Current Anthropology, 28 (1), 63-71.

Halverson, J. (1992). Paleolithic art and cognition. The Journal of Psychology, 126 (3), 221-236.

Harding, J. (1976). Certain Upper Palaeolithic Venus' statuettes considered in relation to the pathological condition known as massive hypertrophy of the breasts. Man, 11(1), 271-272.

Harrington, S. P. M. (1999). Human footprints at Chauvet cave. Archaeology: Newsbriefs 52(5).[Online] Available: http://

www.archeology.org/9909newsbriefs/chauvet.html

Hartmann, E. (1999, March). The nature and uses of dreaming. USA Today,127 (2646), 64-66.

Hayden, B. (1993). The cultural capacities of Neanderthals: A review and re-evaluation. Journal of Human Evolution, 24(2), 113-146.

Henshilwood, C. S., d'Errico, F., Yates, R., Jacobs, Z., Tribolo, C., Duller, G. A., Mercier, N., Sealy, J. C., Valladas, H., Watts, I., & Wintle, A. C. (2002). Emergence of modern human behavior: Middle Stone Age engravings from South Africa. Science, 295, 1278-1280.

Holden, C. (1999). Ancient child uncovered in Portugal. AAAS Science News Service. [On-line].Available:http://www. academicpress.com/insight/01041999/grapha.htm

Horton, R. & Finneagan, R. (1973). Modes of thought. London: Faber & Faber. Http://www.culture.fr.culture/archeosm/en/ cosqu2.htm

Human Antiquity Update Archive. [On-line]. Available: http: // www.anthropology.ccsu.edu/human_antiquity/ARCHIVES/ archive_chapter14.htm

Hyland, M. (1993). Size of human groups during the Paleolithic and the evolutionary significance of increased group size. Behavioral and Brain Sciences, 16(4), 709-710.

Iberian rock art of the Mediterranean basin. (1999). [On-line]. Available:http://www.tourspain.es/turespa/lupatri3.htm.

Irwin, A. (2000). The hooked stick in the Lascaux shaft scene. Antiquity, 74(284), 293-298.

Jacoby, J. (1998). Scientists don't agree on global warming. [On-ine]. Available: http:// www.bigeye.com/jj110598.htm.

James, W. (1981). The Principles of psychology. Cambridge, MA: Harvard University Press.

Klein, S. (1990). Human cognitive changes at the Middle to Upper Palaeolithic transition: The evidence of Boker Tachtit. In P. Mellars (Ed.), The emergence of modern humans. (pp. 499-16). Ithaca, NY: Cornell University Press.

Kooijmans, L. P. L. , Smirnov, Y. , Solecki, R. S. , Villa, P., Weber, T. & Gargett, R. H. (1989). On the evidence for Neanderthal burial. Current Anthropology, 30(3), 322-330.

Kuhn, H. (1955). On the the track of prehistoric man. (A. H. Brodrick, Trans.). New York: Random House.

Kurten, B. (1976). The cave bear story. New York: Columbia.

La Barre, W. (1970). The ghost dance, origins of religion. Garden City, NY: Doubleday.

La grotte de Cussac. (2001). [On-line]. Available:http:// www. culture/arcnat/cussac/

Laming, A. (1959). Lascaux paintings and engravings. (E. F. Armstrong, Trans.). Baltimore, MD: Penguin Books.

Leroi-Gourhan, A. (1957). Prehistoric man. New York: Philosophical Library.

Leroi-Gourhan, A. (1967). Treasures of prehistoric art. (N. Guterman, Trans.). New York: Abrams.

Leroi-Gourhan, A. (1982). The dawn of European art. (S. Champion, Trans.). London:Cambridge.

Leroi-Gourhan, A. (1989). The hunters of prehistory. (C. Jacobson, Trans.). New York: Atheneum.

Leroi-Gourhan, A. (1975). The flowers found with Shanidar IV, a Neanderthal burial in Iraq. Science, 190, 562-564.

Lewis- Williams, J. D. & Dawson, T. A. (1988). The signs of all times: entopic phenomena in upper Paleolithic art. Current Anthropology, 29(2), 201-245.

Lewis-Williams, J. D. (1991). Wrestling with analogy: A methodological dilemma in Upper Palaeolithic art research. In A. J. Lawson (Ed.), Proceedings of the Prehistoric Society, 1(57). (pp. 149-162). Great Britain: The Prehistoric Society.

Lewis-Williams, J. D. (1997). Harnessing the brain:Vision and shamanism in upper Paleolithic western Europe. In M. W. Conkey (Ed.), Beyond art: Pleistocene image and symbol. (pp. 321-342). San Francisco: California Academy of Sciences.

Lewis-Williams, J. (1997). Agency, art and altered consciousness: a motif in French (Quercy) upper Palaeolithic art. Antiquity, 7(274), 810-830.

Lietava, J. (1992). Medicinal plants in a Middle Paleolithic grave Shanidar IV? Journal of Pharmacology, 35(3), 263-266.

Lommel, A. (1967). The world of the early hunters. (M. Bullock, Trans.). London: Evelyn, Adams& Mackay.

Lorblanchet, M. (1989). From man to animal and sign in Palaeolithic art. (M. Conkey, Trans.). In H. Murphy (Ed.), Animals Into Art (pp. 21-56). London: Unwin Hyman.

MacErlean, F. (2012). First Neanderthal cave paintings discovered in Spain. [On-line]. Available: http://www.newscientist.com/ article/ dn21458-first-neanderthal-cave-paintings-discovered-in-spain.html

Man of Neanderthal Museum, La Chapelle aux Saints. (2000). [On-line]. Available:http://www.altermed.org/museelcas/pagesgb/ decouvertegeb.html.

Maringer, J. & Bandi, H. G. (1953). Art in the ice age. (R. Allen, Trans.). New York: Prager.

Maringer, J. (1960). The gods of prehistoric man. (M. Ilford, Trans.) New York: Knopf.

Markale, J. (1999). The great goddess:Reverence of the divine feminine from the Paleolithic to the present. (J. Gladding, Trans.) Rochester, VT: Inner Traditions.

Marshack, A. (1976). Some implications of the Paleolithic symbolic evidence for the origin of language. Current Anthropology, 17 (2), 274-282.

Marshack, A. (1981). On Paleolithic ochre and the early uses of color and symbols. Current Anthropology, 22(2), 188-191.

Marshack, A. (1991). The roots of civilization. Mount Kisco, NY: Moyer Bell.

Marshack, A. (1996). Self-representation in upper Paleolithic female figurines. [Comments], Current Anthropology, 37(2), 259-63.

Marshack, A. (1997). Paleolithic image making and symboling in Europe and the Middle East: A comparative review. In M. W. Conkey (Ed.), Beyond art:Pleistocene image and symbol. (pp. 53-91). San Francisco: California Academy of Sciences.

Mazonowicez, D. (1974). A search for cave and canyon art, voices from the stone age. New York: Thomas Y. Crowell.

McCoid, C. &McDermott, L. (1996). Toward decolonizing gender. American Anthropologist, 98 (2), 319-326.

McCrone, J. (1999). Left brain, right brain. New Scientist. [On-line]. Available: http://www.newscientist.com/ns/19990703/ left brainr.html

McDermott, F., Grun, R., Stringer, C. B. & Hawkesworth, C. J.

(1993). Mass-spectrometric U-series dates for Israeli Neanderthal/early modern hominid sites. Nature, 363(6426), 252-255.

McDermott, J. P. (1999). Definitions of religion. [On-line]. Available:http://www.canisius.edu/~mcdermot/relig.html

McDermott, L. C. (1996). Self-representation in upper Paleolithic female figurines. Current Anthropology, 37(2), 227-248.

Mellars, P. (1996). The neanderthal legacy. Princeton, NJ: Princeton University Press.

Mellars, P. (1998). The fate of the Neanderthals. Nature, 395 (6702), 539-540.

Mellars, P. (1998). The Upper Palaeolithic revolution. In B. Cunliffe (Ed.), Prehistoric Europe: An illustrated history (pp. 42-78). Oxford: Oxford University Press.

Mishra, S. (1998). Verification based analogical reasoning. [On-line]. Available:http://www.cc.gatech.edu/people/home/smishra/vbal.html

Mithen, S. (1988). Looking and learning: Upper Palaeolithic art and information gathering. World Archaeology, 19(3), 297-327.

Mithen, S. (1988). To hunt or to paint: Animals and art in the Upper Palaeolithic. Man, 23(4), 671-695.

Mithen, S. (1994). From domain specific to generalized intelligence: a cognitive interpretation of the middle/upper Paleolithic transition. In C. Renfrew & E. Zubrow (Eds.), The ancient mind: Elements of cognitive archaeology (pp. 29-39). Great Britain: Cambridge University Press.

Mithen, S. (1996). Anthropomorphism and the evolution of cognition. The Journal of the Royal Anthropological Institute. 2(4), 717-719.

Mithen, S. (1997). Anthropomorphism and the evolution of cognition. Journal of the Royal Anthropological Institute, 2, 717-719.

Molyneaux, B. L. (1995). The sacred earth. Alexandria, VA: Time-ife Books.

Mondloch, C. J., Lewis, T. L., Budreau, D. R., Maurer, D., Dannemiller, J. L., Stephens, B. R. & Kleiner-Gathercoal, K. A. (1999). Face perception during early infancy. Psychological Science, 10(5), 419-422.

Monick, E. (1987). Sacred image of the masculine. Toronto, Canada: Inner City.

Moulin, R. J. (1965). Prehistoric painting. (A. Rhodes, Trans.). New York: Funk& Wagnells.

Moustakas, C. (1994). Phenomenological research methods. Thousand Oaks, CA: Sage Publications.

Muller, F. M. (1882). Lectures on the origin and growth of religion. London: Longmans Green.

Murray, M. A. (1963). The genesis of religion. London: Routledge & Kegan Paul. Neanderthal Museum. (2000). [On-line]. Available: http://www.neanderthal.de/ethal/pg_40.htm

Nelson, S. M. (1997). Gender in archaeology. London: Altamira Press.

Neugebauer-Maresch, C. (1989). Zum Neufund einer weiblichen Statuette bei den Rettungsgrabungen an der der Aurignacien-tation Stratzing. Germania, 67, 551-60.

News in Science. (2000). [On-line]. Available:http://www. abc. net. au/science/news/print_200504.htm.

Nougier, L. R. (1966). Prehistory: characteristics of Paleolithic art. In the Encyclopedia of world art (Vol. XI, pp. 566-594). New York: McGraw- Hill.

Pericot, L.(1966). The social life of Spanish Paleolithic hunters as shown by Levantine art. In S. L Washburn (Ed.), Social life of early man (pp. 194-213). Chicago: Aldine Publishing.

Pettitt, P. (1999). Neanderthals, sex and modern humans. British Archaeology(45) [On-line]. Available: http://www.Britarch. ac.uk/ba/ba45/bafeat.html

Pfeiffer, J. E. (1982). Creative explosion, an inquiry into the origins of art and religion. New York: Harper&Row.

Pfeiffer, J. E. (1983). The world's first and longest-lived art movement. Smithsonian,14(1), 36-45.

Powell, T. G. E. (1966). Prehistoric art. New York: Frederick A. Praeger.

Prideaux, T. (Ed.). (1973). Cro-magnon man. New York: Time-Life.

Pringle, H. (1998a). New women of the ice age. Discover, 19(4), 62-9.

Pringle, H. (1998b). Neolithic agriculture :The slow birth of agriculture. Science Magazine(282), 1446.

Raphel, M. (1945). Prehistoric cave paintings. (N. Guterman, Trans.). Washington, DC: Pantheon.

Rappaport, R. A. (1999). Ritual and religion in the making of humanity. New York: Cambridge University.

Renfrew, C. (1994). Towards a cognitive archaeology. In C. Renfrew & E. Zubrow (Eds.), The ancient mind:Elements of cognitive archaeology (pp. 3-12). Great Britain: Cambridge University Press.

Renfrew, C. (1994). The archaeology of religion. In C. Renfrew & E. Zubrow (Eds.), The ancient mind:Elements of cognitive archaeology (pp. 47-54). Great Britain: Cambridge University Press.

Rice, P. (1982). Prehistoric Venuses: symbols of motherhood or womanhood? Journal of Anthropological Research, 37(4), 402-414.

Rice, P. C. & Paterson, A. L. (1985). Cave art and bones: Exploring the interrelationships. American Anthropologist, 87(1), 94-100.

Rice, P. C. & Paterson, A. L. (1986). Validating the cave art-archeofaunal relationship in Cantabrian Spain. American Anthropologist, 88(3), 658-667.

Riel-Salvatore, J. & Clark, G. A. (2001). Middle and Early Upper Paleolithic burials and the use of chronotypology in contemporary Paleolithic research. Current Anthropology, 42(4), 449-479.

Ries, J. (1994). The origins of religions. (K. Singleton, Trans.). Grand Rapids, MI: William B. Eerdmans.

Roach, J. (2008). Neanderthals ate dolphins, seals, cave remains suggest. [On-line]. Available: http://news.national geographic .com/news/2008/09/080922-neanderthals-caves.html

Roos, Bram. (Executive Producer). (2000, October). Histories mysteries: The cavemen. History Channel.

Rudgley, R. (1999). The lost civilizations of the stone age. New York: The Free Press.

Ruspoli, M. (1986). The cave of Lascaux. New York: Harry M. Abrams.

Schwarcz, H., Simpson, J. & Stringer, C. (1998). Neanderthal skeleton from Tabun: U-series data by gamma-ray spectrometry. Journal of Human Evolution 35,(6), 635-645.

SciTechDaily. (2014). Caves of Neja contain earliest human drawings. [On-line]. Available: http://scitechdaily.com/caves-of-nerja-contain-earliest-human-drawings/

Sebastion, L., Xu, H., Ko, A., Li, M. Renaud, G., Butthof, A. Schroder, R. Stoneking, M. (2014). Human paternal and maternal demographic histories: insights from high-Resolution Y chromosome and mtDNA sequences. [On-line]. Available: http://www.investigativegenetics. com/content/5/1/13.

Segal, E. M. (1994). Archaeology and cognitive science. In C. Renfrew & E. Zubrow (Eds.), The ancient mind: Elements of cognitive archaeology (pp. 22-28). Great Britain: Cambridge University Press.

Segal, R. A. (1999). Weber and Geertz on the meaning of religion. Religion 29, (1), 61-71.

Shackley, M. (1980). Neanderthal man. Hamden, CT: Archon.

Sharpe, E. J. (1986). Comparative religion: A history. LaSalle, IL: Open Court.

Shreeve, J. (1995). The Neanderthal enigma. New York: Avon Books.

Sieveking, A. (1979). The cave artists. London: Thames and Hudson.

Sieveking, A. (1997). Cave as context in Palaeolithic art. BAR International Series, 667, 25-37.

Sieveking, A. & Sieveking, G. (1966). The caves of France and northern Spain. Philadelphia: Dufour.

Smith, N. W. (1992). An analysis of ice age art. New York: Peter Lang.

Smith, W. C. (1978). The meaning and end of religion. New York: Harper& Row.

Snow, D. R. (2013). Sexual dimorphism in European Upper Paleolithic cave art. American Antiquity. vol. 78, no. 4; doi: 10.7183/0002-7316.78.4.746.

Soffer, O., Adovasio, J. M., & Hyland, D. C. (2000).Textiles, basketry, gender, and status in the Upper Paleolithic. Current Anthropology, 41(4), 511-537.

Soffer, O., Adovasio, J. M., Illingworth, J. S., Amirkhanov, H. A., Praslov, N. D. & Street, M. (2000). Palaeolithic perishables made permanent. Antiquity, 74(286), 812-821.

Solecki, R. S. (1957). Shanidar cave. Scientific American, 197, 58-64.

Solecki, R.S. (1971). Shanidar, the first flower people. New York: Knopf.

Solecki, R. S. (1972). Shanidar, the humanity of Neanderthal man. London: Allen Lane.

Solecki, R.S. (1975). Shanidar IV, a Neanderthal flower burial in northern Iraq. Science, 190, 880-881.

Solecki, R. S. (1975). The middle Paleolithic site of Nahr Ibrahim (Asfourieh Cave) in Lebanon. In F. Wendorf & A. E. Marks (Eds.), Problems in prehistory:North Africa and the Levant (pp. 283-295). Dallas, TX: SMU Press.

The sorcerer of the cave of the three brothers. (1999). [On-line]. Available:http://www.lugodoc.demon.co.uk/sctb.htm

Speth, J. D. & Tchernov, E. (1998). The role of hunting and scavenging in Neanderthal procurement strategies. In T. Akazawa, K. Aoki & O. Bar-Yosef (Eds.), Neanderthals and modern humans in western Asia(pp. 223-239). New York: Plenum Press.

Spilka, B., Hood, R. W. & Gorsuch, R. L. (1985). The psychology of religion, an empirical approach. Englewood Cliffs, NJ: Prentice-Hall.

States, B. O. (1997). Seeing in the dark. New Haven, CT: Yale University Press.

Stringer, C. (2000). Palaeoanthropology: Coasting out of Africa. Nature, 405, 24-27.

Stringer, C. & Gamble, C. (1993). In search of the Neanderthals: Solving the puzzle of human origins. New York: Thames and Hudson.

Sweet, S. J. (1997). Global warming controversy: Heating up. [On-line]. Available: http://mt.wwwcapis.com/features/4f9709 24. html.

Tattersall, I. (1995). Neanderthal: The rise, success, and mysterious extinction of our closest human relatives. New York: MacMillan.

Tattersall, I. (1998). Becoming human. New York: Harcourt Brace.

Than, K. (2012). World's oldest cave art found--made by

Neanderthals? [On-line]. Available:http://news.nationalgeographic.com/news/2012/06/120614-neanderthal-cave-paintings-spain-science-pike/

Travers, M. D. (1996). Animacy and agents. In Programming with agents: New metaphors for thinking about computation. [On-line]. Available:http://mt.www.media.mit.edu/people/mt/thesis /mt-thesis.html.

Tresguerres, J. (1976). Azilian burial from Los Azules I, Asturias, Spain. Current Anthropology, 17(4), 769-770.

Trinkaus, E. (1983). The Shanidar Neanderthals. New York: Academic Press.

Trinkaus, E. & Shipman, P. (1993). The Neanderthals: Changing the image of mankind. New York: Knopf.

Tylor, E. B. (1958). Religion in primitive culture. (Vol. 2). New York: Harper & Row.

Ucko, P. J. & Rosenfeld, A. (1967). Paleolithic cave art. New York: McGraw-Hill.

Valladas, H., Mercier, N., Joron, J. L., & Reyss, J. L. (1998). GIF laboratory dates for middle Paleolithic Levant. In T. Akazawa, K. Aoki & O. Bar-Yosef (Eds.), Neandertals and modern humans in western Asia (pp. 69-75). New York: Plenum Press.

Van de Castle, R. (1994). Our dreaming mind. New York: Ballantine Books.

Velo, J. (1984). Ochre as medicine: A suggestion for the interpretation of the archaeological record. Current Anthropology, 25(2), 674.

Velo, J. (1988). On Paleolithic art. Current Anthropology, 29(2), 309-310.

Vialou, D. (1998). The prehistoric imagination (rock art). UNESCO Courier, 5, 17-20.

Vialou, D. (1998). Prehistoric art and civilization. (P. G. Bahn, Trans.). New York: Harry N. Abrams.

Vidal-Rodriguez, J., d'Errico, F. Pacheco, F. A., Blasco, R. Rosell, J., Jennings, R. P. Queffelec, A., Finlayson, G., Fa, D. A., Lopez, J. M. G., Carrion, J. S., Negro, J. J., Finlayson, S. Caceres, L. M., Bernal, M. A., Jimenez, S. F. A rock engraving made by Neanderthals in Gibraltar. (2014).

[Online] Proceedings of the National Academy of Sciences. Available: http://www.pnas.org/content111/37/13301.

Vila, C., Savolainen, P., Maldonado, J. E., Amorim, I. R., Rice, J. E. Honeycutt, R. L., Crandell, K. A., Lundeberg, J. L. & Wayne, R. K. (1999). Multiple and ancient origins of the domestic dog. [On-line]. Available: http://www.kc.nett/~wolf2dog/wayne1.htm.

Waller, S. J. (1993). Sound and rock art. Nature, 363(6429), 501.

White, R. (1986). Dark caves, bright visions. New York: W. W. Norton.

Witcombe, C. L. C. E. (1998). Women in prehistory, the Venus of Willendorf. [On-line]. Available: http://www.arthistory.sbc.edu/ imageswomen/willendorf discoveryhtml.

Wreschner, E. E. (1976). The red hunters: further thoughts on the evolution of speech. Current Anthropology, 17(4), 717-719.

Wreschner, E. E. (1985). Evidence and interpretation of red ochre in the early prehistoric sequences. In P. Tobias (Ed.), Hominid evolution, past present and future (pp.387-394). New York: Alan R. Liss.

Zervos, C. (1959). L'art epoque du renne en France. Paris: Cahiers D'Art.

Zihlman, A. (1997). The Paleolithic glass ceiling. In L. D Hager (Ed.), Women in human evolution (pp. 91-113). London: Routledge.

www.ingramcontent.com/pod-product-compliance
Lightning Source LLC
LaVergne TN
LVHW020714110826
845149LV00012B/2265

9780990645726